SiMPLY

TOEFL iBT®

Reading & Vocabulary

Based on 6 controversial and interesting issues

including

TOEFL Reading Guide

An **essential** Guide for the **READING** section of the TOEFL Exam, enabling familiarization with the format of the exam as well as with the various types of reading comprehension tasks that are used.

Andrew Betsis
Anthoney Demos
Linda Maria Windsor

GlobalELT
ENGLISH LANGUAGE TEACHING BOOKS

TABLE OF CONTENTS

Published by GLOBAL ELT LTD
www.globalelt.co.uk
Copyright © **GLOBAL ELT LTD, 2014**

Marianna Georgopoulou, Dimitris Primalis, Linda Lethem and Lawrence Mamas have also contributed to this publication.

Every effort has been made to trace the copyright holders and we apologize in advance for any unintentional omission.
We will be happy to insert the appropriate acknowledgements in any subsequent editions.

British Library Cataloguing-in-Publication Data
A catalogue record of this book is available from the British Library.

● Simply TOEFL iBT® - Reading & Vocabulary - Student's Book - ISBN: 9781781640647
● Simply TOEFL iBT® - Reading & Vocabulary - Teacher's Book - ISBN: 9781781640654
● Simply TOEFL iBT® - Reading & Vocabulary - Self-Study Edition - ISBN: 9781781640661

INTRODUCTION

Simply TOEFL iBT® Reading & Vocabulary prepares candidates for the Reading section of the TOEFL iBT® exam.

Rationale

6 debatable issues were selected with the following in mind: candidates in the TOEFL iBT® exam are required to deal with academic issues in the Writing and Speaking sections of the test, taking into account **conflicting ideas**. They are often asked to compare and contrast information they are provided with or agree/disagree with an issue giving reasons for their opinion. It is, therefore, essential for them to be familiar with such type of argumentation. Exposure to conflicting ideas on any given topic is particularly useful for both understanding the texts that are used as '**input**' of information (as is the case with the Reading and Listening sections) as well as for preparing candidates to produce their own ideas ('**output**' of information) in the Writing and Speaking sections of the TOEFL iBT® exam.

Furthermore, research has shown that **debate arouses interest**. By reading the 'pros' or 'cons' in any given issue (in the first Text) the candidates are very likely to be motivated to look forward to reading the 'opposite view' in the second Text, in this book.

Targets

Simply TOEFL iBT® Reading & Vocabulary focuses on **recognition** and **development** of useful VOCABULARY for the TOEFL iBT® test, with an ultimate aim of **building** a wide range of vocabulary through practice.

There are 5 Vocabulary Building Exercises for each paragraph.

* Exercise A is a Multiple Choice activity with 4 possible answers, all of which can be found in the text.
* Exercise B is a Fill-in-the-blanks exercise using words from the text, either as they appear in the text or changed into another form.
* Exercise C is a Matching exercise, where definitions have to be matched with words that, again, appear in the text.
* Exercise D asks candidates to come up with derivatives of words appearing in the text, as well as synonyms and antonyms.
* Exercise E is a productive type of exercise. Candidates are asked to write their own sentences by using words related to the text.

Candidates will also familiarize themselves with the various types of TOEFL-specific reading tasks. Each paragraph of each of the texts is followed by 7 TOEFL-type Reading Comprehension Questions, instead of the usual 2 or 3 that candidates will find at the actual exam. This explains why Text A, in this book, is longer than what is normally expected in the actual TOEFL iBT® exam.

There is a variety of TOEFL-type tasks, with Multiple Choice Questions on:

(1) word meaning
(2) phrase meaning
(3) text meaning: specific information
(4) text meaning: global understanding
(5) inserting a sentence into the text
(6) summarizing the main points of the text, and
(7) filling in a chart with 2 aspects.

Structure

The initial pages provide the candidates with an essential **Guide** for the READING section of the TOEFL iBT® Exam, enabling familiarization with the format of the exam as well as with the various types of reading comprehension tasks that are used.

Next, there are 5 **Debates**. Each Debate consists of two texts (Text A and Text B) presenting conflicting viewpoints on an issue, either in favor or against a viewpoint.

In **Text A**, each paragraph is followed by a series of Vocabulary Building exercises (the 'left' page in each spread) and on the following page, TOEFL-type Reading Comprehension tasks are provided. The reason behind opting for analyzing each paragraph separately and not the text as a whole lies on the realization that for effective vocabulary building, the attention span required has to be considerably smaller and interest has to be aroused in terms of anticipation.

Text B explores views that conflict with the views presented in Text A. It is also followed by both Vocabulary Building and Reading Comprehension questions. However Text B is treated as a whole passage and not as short individual paragraphs.

Following the 5 Debates, there are 40 **Revision** Multiple Choice questions with an aim to revise 160 words.

Lastly, a more challenging 6th Debate is provided with a focus on reading comprehension and TOEFL iBT® **exam practice**.

Extras

Another book in the same TOEFL iBT® exam preparation series, *Simply TOEFL iBT® Writing*, includes writing activities, as well as sample and model essays, related to the same topics and debates; it also makes use of most of the vocabulary presented in this book. With an emphasis on essay writing, it can be used either as a stand-alone book or in conjunction with the *Simply TOEFL iBT® Reading & Vocabulary* book.

Need to Know Essentials
THE READING SECTION

This Guide to the TOEFL Reading section, as well as other similar Guides to the Listening, the Writing and the Speaking sections, can be found in the publication, by Global ELT, entitled SUCCEED IN TOEFL - ADVANCED LEVEL - 6 COMPLETE PRACTICE TESTS

The Bare Facts:
- you will be asked to read **three** to **five passages**
- **each passage** will have **twelve** to **fourteen** comprehension **questions**
- the Reading section will be divided into **two to three** separately-timed parts
- for each part, the clock on the screen will count down and indicate how much time you have left

Preparing:
- read extensively - **read up on a variety of different types of topics** to help build vocabulary
- challenge yourself - **read difficult texts;** this will help you develop skills for coping with a range of academic topics and even sections of text which you find hard to understand
- be selective - **read** up on the kinds of **subjects likely to appear** - the practical sciences, technology, the humanities, social sciences etc.

Exam Day:
Timing
- you will have **between 60 and 100 minutes**
- you must use your time well
- **know the format** of the exam very well before exam day - this will save you a lot of time having to check through the Directions for each part
- the Directions are the same in every version of the test - if you know them, you can click the **Dismiss Directions** button
- answer all the questions and **guess if you don't really know** rather than spending too much time on any one question - there is no negative marking so you will not be penalized for selecting a wrong answer

Tackling each passage
- **read the passage** through first
- the main topic is usually stated toward the beginning - try to identify and understand it
- look for ideas that support the topic and seem important
- do not be concerned with understanding or absorbing every last detail

- **next read each question** carefully
- after you read each question, try to locate where the answer is in the text (you may be told)
- read this section carefully if necessary for better understanding

- **if you cannot answer** a particular question, **skip it**
- answer the rest of the questions for the passage and then come back to the skipped question(s)
- remember: you can skip in the Reading but not in the Listening

---

Reading a Passage (in general)

 read for gist
read the passage through once for a general understanding of the topic and the key points

 skim/scan for content
read the question, then scam or skim the text to identify where the answer is (but only if necessary - in questions where you are shown where the answer is, skip this step)

 read for detail
read the section with the answer carefully if necessary to ensure that you understand it properly and make the right selection

Need to Know Essentials
THE READING SECTION

Question Types
There are four main question types.

Multiple Choice

1
- there are four answer options and only one correct answer
- questions may test comprehension, or require the test-taker to choose a synonym of a word or choose the correct paraphrase of a highlighted section of text

Example:

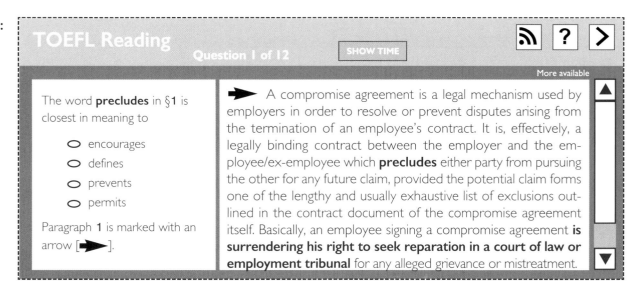

Insert a Sentence

2
- you are given a sentence
- four different points in the passage are marked as possible places where the sentence could go
- you must select the correct place

Example:

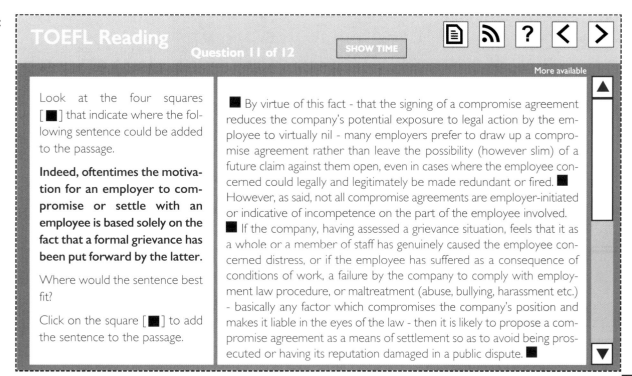

Need to Know Essentials
THE READING SECTION

Question Types
There are four main question types.

3

Summary
- there are five to seven answer choices and you **select** three and **drag** them to the bullet points
- this type of question is **worth more than one point**

Example:

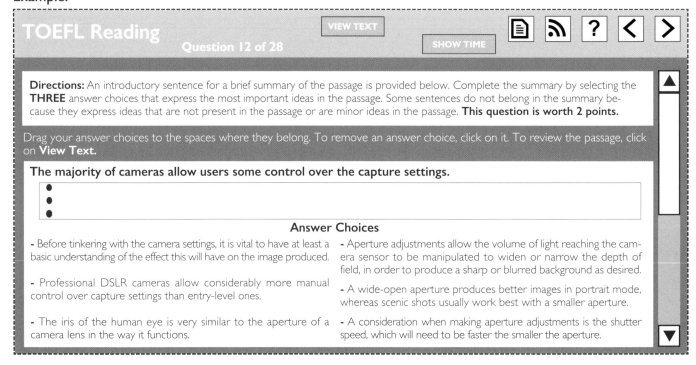

4

Category Chart
- there are five to seven correct answer choices and two categories
- you must drag and drop the answer choices into the correct categories
- not all the answer choices will need to be used

Example:

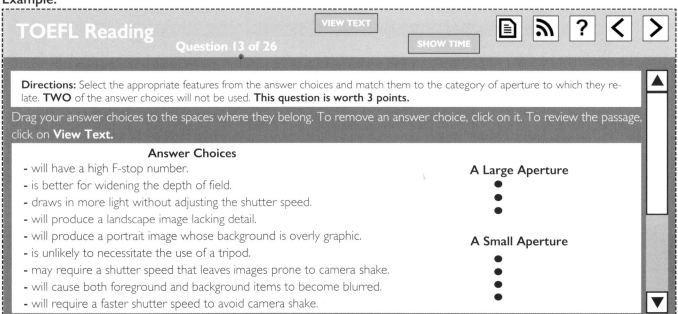

Reading Practice 1
COMPROMISE AGREEMENTS

First, read the passage once over [always start by reading the passage from start to finish and try to understand the topic and key points].

A compromise agreement is a legal mechanism used by employers in order to resolve or prevent disputes arising from the termination of an employee's contract. It is, effectively, a legally binding contract between the employer and the employee/ex-employee which **precludes** either party from pursuing the other for any future claim, provided the potential claim forms one of the lengthy and usually exhaustive list of exclusions outlined in the contract document of the compromise agreement itself. Basically, an employee signing a compromise agreement **is surrendering his right to seek reparation in a court of law or employment tribunal** for any alleged grievance or mistreatment. In return, he will typically receive a sum of compensation, and, in many cases, the guarantee of a good oral or written reference (sometimes both) worded in a manner which has been agreed by the two signatories to the compromise agreement in advance.

It is usually the employer who proposes a compromise agreement. That said, employees are also completely within their rights to suggest **such a mechanism** as a means of settlement of a dispute - though it is rare for discussions on the formation of a compromise agreement to be initiated in this manner. At any rate, if the two parties, employer and employee, have got to the stage at which a compromise agreement is being discussed, this is usually because it is believed that there is no way to resolve the issue concerned so that the employee could remain, long-term, in the pay of his employer.

One of the most common reasons for the drawing up of such an agreement is in a situation where an employee is seriously underperforming and his employer views it as a desirable and proper outcome to have him removed from his position. In order to avoid having to navigate the long and complex legal quagmire that is the disciplinary process, the employer may deem it in the interests of the company for the employee to be extricated as quickly and painlessly as possible from his position, and so may be prepared to offer him some kind of financial incentive to guarantee that the termination of his contract will not be contested or delayed. In such a scenario, the employer is effectively paying off his employee to leave his job. **This** can often prove the most prudent course of action from both a financial and legal perspective even if the employee is incompetent; financially, as it usually takes a minimum of about six months (during which the employee remains on full pay) for a disciplinary process to establish, in a manner that is legally sound, that the employee is sufficiently incompetent to warrant dismissal; legally, because employers who seek to dismiss members of staff often leave themselves open to claims for unfair or constructive dismissal, which, whether or not upheld, cost a great deal by way of legal fees to defend either way. If, on the other hand, they can get the employee to sign a compromise agreement, they can protect themselves against the possibility of having such a dismissal claim made against them.

➤ **A** By virtue of this fact – that the signing of a compromise agreement reduces the company's potential exposure to legal action by the employee to virtually nil – many employers prefer to draw up a compromise agreement rather than leave the possibility (however slim) of a future claim against them open, even in cases where the employee concerned could legally and legitimately be made redundant or fired. **B** However, as said, not all compromise agreements are employer-initiated or indicative of incompetence on the part of the employee involved. **C** If the company, having assessed a grievance situation, feels that it as a whole or a member of staff has genuinely caused the employee concerned distress, or if the employee has suffered as a consequence of conditions of work, a failure by the company to comply with employment law procedure, or maltreatment (abuse, bullying, harassment etc.) – basically any factor which compromises the company's position and makes it liable in the eyes of the law – then it is likely to propose a compromise agreement as a means of settlement so as to avoid being prosecuted or having its reputation damaged in a public dispute. **D**

Typically, the notion of a compromise agreement will first be propositioned in a 'without prejudice' meeting or in a 'without prejudice' document. The term 'without prejudice' is basically legal jargon for 'off the record', and, if discussions are conducted on this basis, it means that any views, positions or proposals put forward in the discussions, and any related documentary evidence, is inadmissible in a court of law. The idea behind the notion of 'without prejudice' is that it encourages openness and honesty, and a situation whereby both sides in the dispute can make known their positions without fear of the consequences. In theory, this creates a better understanding of the situation for both sides, and enables a speedier resolution of the dispute.

In any 'without prejudice' discussions, employees are strongly advised to have legal representation present acting on their behalf or, at the very least, to have sought legal advice on how to proceed and put forward their case prior to commencing discussions. That said, the law does not oblige them to do this. The employee is, however, under obligation to seek out a professional legal opinion before any contract drawn up as part of the compromise agreement is signed. Once the agreement has been signed, the individual is sworn to secrecy and may not reveal the terms to anyone. To do so would be to compromise the compromise agreement so to speak and leave him open to suit by his former employer.

Q1 The word *precludes* in § 1 is closest in meaning to

    A encourages   **B** defines   **C** prevents   **D** permits

[Understanding Meaning] Q1 is an example of a type of question which **tests the reader's understanding of meaning;** in this case, **a synonym must be found.** Even if you do not know the word, you can look for clues from the context of the question-word in the text, so read the section of text directly before and after the question-word carefully (and read the entire paragraph if necessary to help you understand what message the writer is trying to convey). Here, for example, the first line tells us that compromise agreements are designed to stop disputes from happening, which gives us a clue as to whether a suitable verb here should have a negative or positive meaning, just as does the preposition "from", which is used here in association with "precludes".

Q2 In stating that an employee who signs a compromise agreement *is surrendering his right to seek reparation in a court of law or employment tribunal*, the author means that the signing of a compromise agreement

    A marks the beginning of court proceedings brought by an employee.

    B is done in a court or tribunal if requested by an employee.

    C is done by an employee after a court or tribunal has ended.

    D stops an employee from taking further action in a court or tribunal.

[Understanding Meaning] Q2 is a further example of a type of question which **tests the reader's understanding of meaning;** in this case, **your understanding of a whole sentence, clause or phrase** is being tested, rather than just your understanding of a single word. First, read the highlighted text and the text directly before and after it. It may help you to try to put the highlighted text in context and then to paraphrase it in your own words. This should help you to better understand what the writer is trying to say, and, at the same time, will also help you to select the right answer, which will also be a form of paraphrase of the original statement or term contained in the highlighted text.

Q3 The phrase *such a mechanism* in § 2 refers to

    A a compromise agreement

    B the disciplinary procedure

    C a way of raising a grievance

    D a rare form of dispute

Q4 The word *this* in Line 7 of § 3 refers to

    A a type of guarantee

    B paying off the employee

    C leaving the job

    D taking paid leave from the job

[Locating Referents] Qs 3 and 4 are examples of questions which require you to locate referents. A referent is a **word or phrase to which the highlighted question-word or question-phrase refers.** For example, in the sentence "The man and woman arrived at the venue to meet up with Tara as agreed, though she was nowhere to be seen", the referent of "she" is "Tara".

Q5 The author seems to suggest that

    A following the correct procedure in order to fire a bad worker is not always the most practical option for employers.

    B carrying out the disciplinary process correctly will protect employers from having to incur legal expenses for unfair dismissal claims.

    C compromise agreements often lead to claims for unfair or constructive dismissal.

    D compromise agreements typically cost a lot by way of legal fees and as a result of having to continue paying the salary of the employee concerned.

[Making Inferences and Drawing Conclusions] Q5 requires you to make an inference based on what the author says in the second half of § 3. Although the author does not explicitly say any of A-D, it is possible to find the correct answer based on the evidence of what he does say - this is what inference is all about.

Q6 The risk of exposure to a lawsuit by an incompetent former employee who has been fired

A is one which decreases the likelihood of companies offering pay-offs to employees who are being let go.

B is considered unlikely enough as to be one which most companies tend not to be too concerned about.

C is one an employer entering into a compromise agreement must be prepared to assume.

D means that many companies are willing to give employees being let go a pay-off which guarantees there will be no claim made against them at a future date.

> **[Making Inferences and Drawing Conclusions]** Q6 is another example of a question where the answer will not be explicitly stated in the text. However, the evidence drawn from what is said in lines 1-5 of § 4 will lead us to choose the correct option.

Q7 The following sentence can be added to § 4:

Indeed, oftentimes the motivation for an employer to compromise or settle with an employee is based solely on the fact that a formal grievance has been put forward by the latter.

§ 4 is marked with an arrow [➡] . Look at the four squares [■] that indicate where the sentence could be added. Where would the sentence best fit? Choose the letter of the square where the sentence should be added.

> **[Understanding the Organization of Ideas]** Q7 is an example of the **insert a sentence** type of task. This type of question requires you to read the surrounding information carefully to decide the best fit, both from a grammatical and semantic (in terms of meaning) point of view. In this particular instance, the use of the word 'indeed' is a big clue as it suggests that the sentence should follow a similar point that has already been made in order to back up or emphasize that point. It is important to understand transitional expressions (like 'indeed') and their functions for such task-types as this [see the table of transitional expressions below]. Another important factor in determining where the sentence should be inserted is often the presence of a pronoun or short phrase that must have a corresponding referent. The position of the referent in the text will play a big part in determining your choice of answer option.

Transitional Expressions

Word function	Example Words	Notes
to qualify	but, however, yet, although, that said...	comes after a related point, making it less strong or positive
to emphasize	indeed, certainly, above all...	comes after a related point, making it stronger or more positive
to illustrate	for example, for instance, such as...	exemplifies a point which it follows
to contrast	on the other hand, whereas, in contrast...	provides a different point of view to the statement it follows
to concede	nevertheless, nonetheless, of course...	contradicts the previous point somewhat by admitting something else
to conclude (to introduce)	finally, in conclusion (firstly, first of all)...	the last (first) point in a sequence or a summary of what has been said
to add	furthermore, moreover, in addition	an additional point related to the last one
to compare	similarly, in the same way...	complements a previous related point
to explain	furthermore, in fact, now...	explains or provides further info on a statement just made
to state a consequence	therefore, consequently, otherwise	outlines a result of a point just made (or, in the case of words like 'otherwise', what will happen if something is not done)

Reading Practice 2
Web 2.0

First, read the passage once over [always start by reading the passage from start to finish and try to understand the topic and key points].

Web 2.0 is a term which was coined in the last decade of the previous century to describe websites which utilise web-based content in a manner far more complex and interactive than the original static-page format of the Internet intended. Not so much a new version of the Internet as the name implies, Web 2.0 is, rather, a reflection of new ways in which software engineers and end-users have learned to exploit existing web technology.

At the chalkface, Web 2.0 is very much in vogue – to the extent now that any classroom where such technology is not utilized is derided for its backwardness; and any teacher not properly versed in the ways of the web lambasted for their inadequateness for the role of modern educator, to be capable for which, it is assumed, you must be completely tech-savvy. There can be no doubt that a good working knowledge of computers and a familiarity with Web 2.0 is desirable; however, that it is critical to quite the extent the importance attributed to it would suggest is a questionable claim indeed. And the problem is, in the euphoria of our (teachers') positively exuberant embrace of Web 2.0, the core skill set that defines a good teacher, and the development and honing of same, have, by and large, been neglected; such that while new teachers may be techies, they – many of them, at least – may also lack the basic competencies required to effectively conduct lessons, manage individual students and student groups, and do all those things which have always been and will always remain essential qualities of an effective teacher; attributes that are neither influenced nor enhanced by the presence, or otherwise, of technology in the classroom.

Indeed, it may well be that this huge shift in focus toward technology has served only to sidetrack us away from focusing on the most important teacher virtues, while at the same time providing a smokescreen for the tech-savvy but otherwise incompetent teacher, who can hide her ineptitude quite literally behind the pixelated screen of excess that is the modern technology-based classroom, with its fancy 48-inch interface.

The trouble is that just as misery loves company, so too does incompetence love to have its confidants – the mediocre mass together. And in this mass mess of technologically-driven mediocrity, the classroom will soon have been usurped by the techno phonies, whose mastery of the virtual world is increasingly being mistaken for and appraised as some sort of sign of general effectiveness as a teacher.

Meanwhile, the genuine real-deal, old-school professionals are being pushed out the door to make way for these web-obsessed whippersnappers – and all in the name of progress. Soon, the classroom will be one big news stream of Internet nonsense; a place vacant of any real substance at all, where children will learn not from Teacher, but from sentence-long tweets and mistake-ridden blogs that require an attention span roughly equivalent to that of a goldfish.

I submit that we must urgently seek to strip it all down, simplify and get back to basics. Teachers are not defined by their technological **adroitness** – far from it – and the sooner we stop filling their heads with notions to the contrary, the sooner education will cease to be a term to which only lip-service is paid any more and will, at long last, become meaningful on a far more profound level once again. It's time for the professionals to reclaim the teaching profession.

Q1 According to the passage, Web 2.0 is

A new methods of using existing technology.

B a completely new form of computer hardware.

C an updated version of the original Internet.

D a new form of complex interactive technology.

[**Understanding Details**] Q1 is an example of a **fact-finding task.** Unless you are told in which section/paragraph to look, this type of question requires you to skim/scan through the passage looking for the section where the information can be found. Once the relevant section has been located, you should read it carefully to make sure you get the right answer. You might consider scanning the text for key words or phrases such as 'Web 2.0' or 'Internet' or 'technology' to help you find the relevant section of text. In more difficult questions, you may also have to skim the passage for general concepts (locating several sections of information to read carefully before finally identifying the relevant one). Remember that the location of the relevant information will be guided somewhat by the question you are answering. For example, if you have just answered a question related to § 3, then you know that the answer to the question you are now on will be found after the point at which you found the answer to the previous question in the passage i.e. later in § 3 or in a subsequent §.

Q2 The passage suggests that the following statements are true of teachers who are very comfortable with using technology EXCEPT

> **A** Their technological knowledge is indicative of how capable they are at conducting good lessons.
> **B** Their familiarity with Web 2.0 is a desirable teacher trait.
> **C** Their familiarity with technology does not necessarily enhance their effectiveness as a teacher.
> **D** Their enthusiasm for embracing technology is shared by many of their peers.

[Understanding Details] Q2 is an example of an **exceptions** task, which is a bit like a fact-finding task in reverse. You are not required to find one true fact in the presence of three false ones as in a traditional fact-finding task. Instead, you must identify the one false fact where three true ones are present. The process is very similar here to fact-finding in terms of tackling the task. Where you are not told to which section/paragraph the question relates, you should scan /skim the passage until you have identified where the information you need is located. Key words/phrases such as 'Web 2.0', should be scanned for, and key concepts such as the notion of "being good at conducting lessons" should be skimmed for if necessary. It often helps to paraphrase the statements in your own words to give you a better understanding of what you are looking to confirm or rule out.

Q3 Which sentence best expresses the essential information highlighted in the passage?

> **A** Over-focusing on technology prevents us from giving sufficient recognition to key teaching attributes and provides poor teachers with a place to hide.
> **B** Inept teachers can no longer hide as they are exposed by the shift in focus towards a technology-led classroom.
> **C** The use of technology in classrooms creates a potential fire hazard in the hands of incompetent or technologically-ignorant teachers.
> **D** The shift in focus toward technology means that before long all classrooms will be able to enjoy the benefits of sharply-pixelated widescreens.

[Understanding Details] Q3 is an example of a **statement-matching** task, where you must identify the statement, A, B, C or D, which most closely matches the highlighted information in meaning in the passage. The statement will generally summarize or simplify the highlighted text. Again, it is useful to paraphrase the highlighted information in the text in your own words to help you to get a better understanding of what is being said. It may also be necessary for you to carefully read the surrounding text to better understand the author's point in context.

Q4 The author appears to suggest that

> **A** the use of technology by teachers in classrooms is making the learning process more miserable for students.
> **B** there are a lot of incompetent teachers clubbing together in support of the notion that technology is vitally important in the classroom.
> **C** mistakes made by those teachers using technology are not as serious as mistakes made by those who are not, since the former are made in the virtual world.
> **D** the mistakes made by teachers who are not knowledgeable about technology are usually less serious than the mistakes made by those that are.

[Understanding Details] Q4 is an example of a task which requires you to **locate restated information** in the passage. This is a bit like a fact-finding task, only there is usually much more information to process than a simple fact. If you are not told where the statements are located in the passage, then they will usually have a theme in common to help you skim the text to identify the relevant section. Or indeed, you may be able to scan for key words or skim for key concepts. Here, for example, we find that the answer is located in § 4. Scanning for the word "miserable" from Option A gives us a clue as we find the similar idea of "misery" in § 4. Skimming for the concept of "clubbing together" in Option B also draws us to the same paragraph, where we find the similar phrase 'mass together'. Scanning for the key phrase 'virtual world' from Option C, also points us to § 4, and so on...

Q5 The word *adroitness* in Paragraph 6 is closest in meaning to

> **A** expertise   **B** qualities   **C** delivery   **D** methods

[Understanding Meaning] Q5 is another example of a Synonym-finding task, similar to Q1 of Reading Practice 1.

Reading Practice 3
Adjusting your Camera Settings for Optimal Results

First, read the passage once over [always start by reading the passage from start to finish and try to understand the topic and key points].

All cameras beyond the most basic models available will allow some degree of manual control over the capture settings. DSLR cameras, be they the entry-level ones we will be using, or the professional DSLRs that are the staple of career photographers, allow the user considerably more say in how scenes are set and captured. However, the ability to manually control one's shots in itself does not assure the photographer of better results. Indeed, in the hands of an unskilled amateur, a camera set in anything other than point-and-shoot mode can be a very uncooperative thing; the likely result being images which are skewed and awkward at best, or, at worst, shots so distorted as to be rendered fit only for hasty deposition in the waste-paper basket. There is more to photography than meets the eye, you see – and no pun intended. So before we go about experimenting with manual settings, it is vital that we have at least some degree of understanding of how adjusting the various capture options, both individually and more than one at a time, will alter the image in our viewfinder. Otherwise, our alterations are unlikely to enhance the scene, and will be about as scientific and sophisticated as the PSP (point, shoot and pray) method, which is simply hit-or-miss at the best of times. Let us now, then, look at some of the basic settings which our DSLRs will allow us to manipulate.

Aperture

Aperture is one half of the exposure equation, the other being Shutter Speed. Control over the former allows you to determine the depth of field of a photograph, with subtle adjustments in same offering you the chance to convey mood, draw attention to a particular point of interest on the image, and influence color and tone. At its simplest, the aperture can be thought of as to the camera lens what the pupil is to the iris of the human eye. In much the same way as the size of the pupil determines how much light gets into the eye, the aperture of a camera lens controls the amount of light that is allowed to reach the camera sensor. The camera lens-iris diaphragm is constructed of metal leaves that open and close to create whatever size of aperture the user desires. Aperture is measured in F-stops, with the smallest F number on the camera lens, rather confusingly perhaps, representing the largest aperture, and the largest F number, the smallest. Although this may appear somewhat counter-logical, the rationale behind an F/2 aperture being larger than an F/8 is actually quite sound. These numbers are, in fact, fractions arrived at by dividing the focal length of the lens by the diameter measurement of the aperture.

A large aperture has the effect of reducing the depth of field, giving background information a blurred quality. Contrariwise, a small aperture, which draws in less light, will put the entire image into better focus, giving a sharper overall look and providing much more detail of what is in the background of the image. For portraits, where the aim is to draw attention to the main subject of the image, a wide-open aperture can prove highly effective in softening the detail of the surrounds. For landscape shots, stopping down is preferable.

Remember that aperture is measured in F-stops. Stopping down refers to selecting a very high F-stop measure in order to maintain depth of field and the overall sharpness of an image. Essentially, you are holding focus from foreground to background to produce a graphic composition. Bear in mind, however, that the smaller the aperture is, the more light it will need to be exposed to. This will require a longer (slower) shutter speed. The longer the shutter speed gets, the greater the likelihood is that camera shake will become an issue. Therefore, for very long shutter speeds, it may be necessary to use a tripod to ensure that your shot is not **spoiled**.

Shutter Speed

The Shutter is located just in front of the camera sensor and controls the length of time **it** is exposed to the light that is entering through the aperture. Shutter Speeds are measured in steps, with each step either halving or doubling the length of exposure. For example, 1/125 allows twice the amount of light in through the lens as 1/250 does, and half the amount of light as 1/60.

Q1 An introductory sentence for a brief summary of the passage is provided below. Complete the summary by selecting the **THREE** answer choices that express the most important ideas in the passage. Some sentences do not belong in the summary because they express ideas that are not present in the passage or are minor ideas in the passage.

The majority of cameras allow users some control over the capture settings.

A	Before tinkering with the camera settings, it is vital to have at least a basic understanding of the effect this will have on the image produced.
B	Professional DSLR cameras allow considerably more manual control over capture settings than entry-level ones.
C	The iris of the human eye is very similar to the aperture of a camera lens in the way it functions.
D	Aperture adjustments allow the volume of light reaching the camera sensor to be manipulated to widen or narrow the depth of field, in order to produce a sharp or blurred background as desired.
E	A wide-open aperture produces better images in portrait mode, whereas scenic shots usually work best with a smaller aperture.
F	A consideration when making aperture adjustments is the shutter speed, which will need to be faster, the smaller the aperture.

[**Summaries and Charts**] Q1 is an example of a **summary-type** task. The purpose of the summary is to outline key or main points. Therefore, there are three possible ways to help you identify the wrong answers: (1) The way the information is expressed in the answer statement is not the same as it is expressed in the passage and the meaning is, therefore, also not the same. [For example, Option B is not actually stated in the passage. Rather, it is said that DSLR cameras in general have this advantage over other camera types.] (2) The information in the answer statement is not representative of a key or main point. [For example, even if Option B was true, it is hardly one of the key points of the passage, which focuses on the importance of understanding capture settings and how adjusting same can affect the type of image produced.] (3) The answer statement simply functions as a distractor, i.e. the passage contains no information about this statement at all or the statement is contradicted by the information in the passage.

This question is basically testing your gist (overall) understanding of the passage - how well you have grasped the key points. Read over the entire passage again if necessary and if time allows (though it is always a good idea to take note of the key points during your first gist-reading at the start of the exercise - then you may not need to read it a second time). Once again, it is useful to try to paraphrase the answer statements in your own words to help you better understand them. Don't be too quick to assume that because an answer statement contains key words from the passage it must be a right answer. The meaning of the statement may not reflect the context in which the key words were used in the passage (careful reading of the relevant section of the passage may be required to confirm either way). Or the point may be a minor one that should not be included in the summary.

Q2 To which type of aperture, large or small, does each statement, A-I, relate? **TWO** of the answer choices will **NOT** be used.

Answer Choices

A will have a high F-stop number.
B is better for widening the depth of field.
C draws in more light without adjusting the shutter speed.
D will produce a landscape image lacking detail.
E will produce a portrait image whose background is overly graphic.
F is unlikely to necessitate the use of a tripod.
G may require a shutter speed that leaves images prone to camera shake.
H will cause both foreground and background items to become blurred.
I will require a faster shutter speed to avoid camera shake.

A large aperture:
- C
- D
- F

A small aperture:
- A
- B
- E
- G

[**Summaries and Charts**] Q2 is an example of a **chart-type** task. These tasks are a bit like fact-finding tasks, but you have to find and confirm several different facts rather than just one. You will need to scan for key words and phrases, and skim for key content. It makes sense to scan for sections which deal with the terms 'large aperture' and 'small aperture' in the text first. Then, starting with Option A, an obvious key term to search for would be 'F-stop'. Similarly, in B, 'depth of field' seems like an obvious choice. Try to search for key words or terms that are technical and cannot be paraphrased, such as the examples just given, as well as terms like 'camera shake', 'tripod', 'portrait image' and so on. Remember that once you have located the relevant information in the passage, it may be necessary to read carefully for detailed understanding. It is also important to note that there will be some wrong answers or distractors that are inserted to confuse you, and which do not need to be classified at all.

Q3 The word **spoiled** in Paragraph 4 is closest in meaning to
A improved   **B** exposed   **C** ruined   **D** repeated

Q4 The word **it** in Line 1 of Paragraph 5 refers to
A the shutter
B the camera sensor
C the time
D the aperture

Q5 A 1/500 step allows
A twice the amount of light in as a 1/250.
B three times the amount of light in as a 1/125.
C half the amount of light in as a 1/250.
D one third the amount of light in as a 1/125.

Debate I

Music Education

Paragraph 1

Researchers, teachers and parents have all **debated** the **validity** of children taking time to learn music either in **formal** classroom **settings** or **privately**. Some experts believe it is a **waste** of **valuable** classroom time, as the **marketplace** traditionally does not value this **abstract** skill. These so-called experts, though, **underestimate** the value of music education that cannot be **measured empirically**. **Regardless** if your child has career **ambitions** in music or not, some form of musical education will **benefit** them. Studies have found that learning music **enables** students to more easily **grasp** other academic subjects and enhance their skills for other uses. Singing, listening, playing and dancing have shown to **markedly** improve the social and academic performance of children from their youth throughout their childhood. **Ultimately**, the child develops various skill sets **concurrently** that provide them with an **edge** both in the classroom and in life.

Vocabulary Building

Exercise A: Choose the option (**a**, **b**, **c** or **d**) which fits best each sentence.

1. The invitation to the gala specified .... attire.
   - **a.** regardless
   - **b.** formal
   - **c.** valuable
   - **d.** abstract

2. An exhibition was held .... with the conference.
   - **a.** concurrently
   - **b.** ultimately
   - **c.** empirically
   - **d.** markedly

Exercise B: Fill in the blanks in the following sentences using words from the box below. There are 2 extra words in the box you do not need to use. You cannot change the words.

| **a.** debate | **b.** underestimate | **c.** measure | **d.** benefit | **e.** enable | **f.** grasp |

1. Both sides will ....benefit........ from the talks.
2. I think you don't ....grasp........ the importance of the matter.
3. You should never ..underestimate.. your opponent before the battle.
4. The workers went on to ....measure........ the height of the ceiling.

Exercise C: Fill in the definitions using words from the box below. There are 2 extra words in the box that you do not need to use.

| **a.** validity | **b.** setting | **c.** waste | **d.** marketplace | **e.** ambition | **f.** edge |

1. ....Edge........ means an advantage; a margin of superiority.
2. ....Validity........ is the quality of something being well-grounded; just.
3. ....Ambition........ is a strong desire to achieve something.
4. ....Setting........ refers to the environment a situation takes place.

Exercise D: Fill in the chart with the derivatives of the given adjectives or adverbs. Then, provide one **synonym** and one **antonym**, taking into account their meaning in the specific text above.

	Verb	Noun	Adjective	Adverb
1.	value	value	valuable	valuably
2.	abstract	abstractness	abstract	abstractly
3.	mark	marking	marked	markedly
4.	concur	concurrence	concurrent	concurrently

		Synonym	Antonym
1.	valuable	important/priceless	useless/worthless/unimportant
2.	abstract	theoretical	concrete
3.	markedly	clearly/obviously	unremarkably/slightly
4.	concurrently	simultaneously/jointly	separately/independently

Exercise E: Write 4 sentences using the following words: useless, slightly, concrete, independently. You must write 1 sentence for each of these words. Use between 8 and 15 words in each sentence.   (Suggested Answers)

1. This manual is useless; it hasn't helped me at all to understand.
2. Well, this model is slightly different from the previous one.
3. I think I need a concrete example to get your theory.
4. We will go on with the project independently of its results.

Music Education

Paragraph 1

A Researchers, teachers and parents have all debated the **validity** of children taking time to learn music either in formal classroom settings or privately. Some experts believe it is a waste of valuable classroom time, as the marketplace traditionally does not value this abstract skill. **B** These so-called experts, though, underestimate the value of music education that cannot be measured empirically. Regardless if your child has career ambitions in music or not, some form of musical education will benefit them. Studies have found that learning music enables students to more easily grasp other academic subjects and enhance their skills for other uses. **C** Singing, listening, playing and dancing have shown to markedly improve the social and academic performance of children from their youth throughout their childhood. **D** Ultimately, the child develops various skill sets concurrently that provide them with an edge both in the classroom and in life.

Reading Comprehension

1. The word **validity** in §1 is closest in meaning to
   a. falseness.
   b. relation.
   c. soundness.
   d. ineffectiveness.

2. According to the passage, why do some think music education should not be taught in schools?
   a. Children don't find the subject interesting.
   b. Parents think it costs too much.
   c. The modern economy doesn't value it enough.
   d. The job market needs more musically inclined people.

3. Why does the author disagree with the critics of music education?
   a. Because learning music and art detracts from a student's social skills.
   b. Because music and art education increases student performance.
   c. Because music and art education takes too much time to learn.
   d. Because music and art education has become an obsolete practice.

4. Which sentence below best expresses the essential information in the underlined sentence in §1?
   a. Detractors of music education need to look beyond rigid measurements to evaluate the benefits of the practice.
   b. Detractors of music education are justified in their arguments against music education.
   c. Critics of music education have been proven right by test scores.
   d. Critics of art and music education have not done enough concrete research on the matter.

5. All of the following have improved the academic and social performance of students **EXCEPT**
   a. singing along with an opera singer.
   b. listening to classical music.
   c. moving to jazz tunes.
   d. memorizing abstract lessons.

6. Look at the four squares, **A**, **B**, **C** and **D**, which indicate where the following sentence could be added to the passage. Where would the sentence best fit?

   Right Answer: B

   Many employers, for example, value hard math and science skills that are necessary to compete in the digital age.

7. An introductory sentence for a brief summary of the passage is provided below. Complete the summary by selecting the **THREE** answer choices that express the most important ideas in the passage. Some sentences do not belong in the summary because they express ideas that are not presented in the passage or are ideas of minor importance. **This question is worth 2 points.**

   Music and art education in schools defies critics, for it enriches students academically and socially.

   a. Students who focus strictly on math and science thrive socially.
   b. Art and music enhance students' ability to learn other subjects.
   c. Studying fine arts has benefits that are not easily measured.
   d. Science should be stressed instead of spending time on drawing courses.
   e. Fine arts equip students with skills and sensitivity that help them in life.

Debate I

Music Education

Paragraph 2
One of the skills music **enhances** for children is their **ability** to **acquire** language, whether it be their native tongue or a **foreign** one. For children nine years old and younger, music has proved to be **invaluable** in **accelerating** their ability to learn more than one language. Music education has proven to help kids **decode** words, sounds, and signals that **facilitate** their ability to learn naturally. Music, in other words, **applies**, **reinforces** and celebrates the **necessary** skills that aid a child in developing their language **capacities**. Studies have shown the **effect** of learning music on the human brain itself. Namely, music education physically **emboldens** the left side of a child's brain where much of language **processing** is focused, whereby music **exposure** helps to **wire** the **circuits** of the brain in a way to enhance their **effectiveness**. Moreover, the **dynamic** between music and language benefits kids socially, for **fluency** with language is the root of social **acumen**. Thus, exposure to music makes it more likely for a child to **possess** formidable **verbal** and written **communication** skills.

Vocabulary Building

Exercise A: Choose the option (**a**, **b**, **c** or **d**) which fits best each sentence.

1. The government decided to .... its privatization program to be finished sooner.
   a. enhance   c. facilitate
   b. accelerate   d. reinforce

2. The .... of computers as an educational tool is confirmed.
   a. ability   c. dynamic
   b. capacity   d. effectiveness

Exercise B: Fill in the blanks in the following sentences using words from the box below. There are 2 extra words in the box you do not need to use. You cannot change the words.

a. acquire	b. possess	c. decode	d. apply	e. wire	f. embolden

1. We can only solve the problem if we ....apply.......... a theory to it.
2. You will soon ....acquire.......... proficiency in English.
3. The experts managed to ....decode.......... the secret documents.
4. He is said to ....possess.......... a huge fortune.

Exercise C: Fill in the definitions using words from the box below. There are 2 extra words in the box that you do not need to use.

a. processing	b. exposure	c. fluency	d. acumen	e. effect	f. circuit

1. ....Fluency.......... is skillfulness in speaking or writing.
2. ....Processing.......... means a series of operations performed in the treatment of a phenomenon.
3. ....Exposure.......... refers to an act of being subjected to an action or its influence.
4. ....Effect.......... is something brought about by a cause; a result.

Exercise D: Fill in the chart with the derivatives of the given adjectives or adverbs. Then, provide one **synonym** and one **antonym**, taking into account their meaning in the specific text above.

	Verb	Noun	Adjective	Adverb			Synonym	Antonym
1.	foreignize	foreignness	foreign	foreignly	1.	foreign	alien/unfamiliar	native
2.	value	value	invaluable	invaluably	2.	invaluable	priceless	worthless/valueless
3.	necessitate	necessity	necessary	necessarily	3.	necessary	essential/indispensable	unnecessary
4.	verbalize	verbalization	verbal	verbally	4.	verbal	spoken	written

Exercise E: Write 4 sentences using the following words: written, unnecessary, native, worthless. You must write 1 sentence for each of these words. Use between 8 and 15 words in each sentence. (Suggested Answers)

1. We will need written evidence if we are to believe you.
2. The slaughter of whales is not simply unnecessary; it is greatly inhuman.
3. French is not my native tongue but I am proficient.
4. The painting was worthless because it was a fake.

Music Education

Paragraph 2

One of the skills music enhances for children is their ability to acquire language, whether it be their native tongue or a foreign one. **A** For children nine years old and younger, music has proved to be invaluable in accelerating their ability to learn more than one language. **B** Music education has proven to help kids decode words, sounds and signals that facilitate their ability to learn naturally. Music, in other words, applies, reinforces and celebrates the necessary skills that aid a child in developing their language capacities. Studies have shown the effect of learning music on the human brain itself. Namely, music education physically **emboldens** the left side of a child's brain where much of language processing is focused, whereby music exposure helps to wire the circuits of the brain in a way to enhance their effectiveness. **C** Moreover, the dynamic between music and language benefits kids socially, for fluency with language is the root of social acumen. **D** Thus, exposure to music makes it more likely for a child to possess formidable verbal and written communication skills.

Reading Comprehension

1. The word **emboldens** in §2 is closest in meaning to
   a. enhances.
   b. weakens.
   c. undermines.
   d. tests.

2. Based on the passage, what is the skill that music education helps a student build?
   a. to memorize spelling words
   b. to develop communication skills
   c. to solve engineering and computer problems
   d. to compose original classical music compositions

3. Why does the author cite scientific research to support his argument?
   a. to show that studying music makes a child's brain smaller
   b. to illustrate how studying math increases the left side of a student's brain
   c. to debunk the theory that music hurts a child's overall development
   d. to show how music helps develop the brain and the subsequent skills

4. Which sentence below best expresses the essential information in the underlined sentence in §2?
   a. By developing communication skills through music students interact socially at a higher level.
   b. By studying music students regress socially and are left unprepared for life.
   c. By enhancing communication skills students no longer need to study art or music.
   d. By developing music skills students lose their ability to relate to their contemporaries over time.

5. Through music education, students have improved all of the following **EXCEPT**
   a. recognizing words.
   b. left brain function.
   c. understanding sounds.
   d. estimating written exams.

6. Look at the four squares, **A**, **B**, **C** and **D**, which indicate where the following sentence could be added to the passage. Where would the sentence best fit?

   Right Answer: C

   Research has yet to determine the total impact on the right side of the brain, but there is potential for intriguing findings.

7. An introductory sentence for a brief summary of the passage is provided below. Complete the summary by selecting the **THREE** answer choices that express the most important ideas in the passage. Some sentences do not belong in the summary because they express ideas that are not presented in the passage or are ideas of minor importance. **This question is worth 2 points.**

   Studying music has proved to enhance brain development and related skills.

   a. Music education has shown to increase the left side of the brain.
   b. Part of the brain, enhanced by music, results in superior communication skills.
   c. Music education has shown to decrease the size of the brain hurting language development.
   d. Fine arts training helps children to express and retain information more easily.
   e. The brain experiences little benefit cognitively from exposure to music lessons.

Debate I

Music Education

Paragraph 3

Music education has also **demonstrated** the **ability** to **augment** a student's IQ. **Studies** have **illustrated** **significant increases** in the IQ of children who have music education versus those that don't. Students in the study who took weekly voice and piano lessons for a nine-month **stretch performed** better on **intelligence** tests than those that didn't **receive** such music education, where their IQs were tested before and after the **training**. **Specifically**, the students who received music classes tested three **points** higher than those who didn't take the classes. Furthermore, these students demonstrated **superior social behavior** skills than those that didn't take such **courses**. Students who also took drama and theater classes during this stretch demonstrated **similar enhanced** IQ and skill sets.

Vocabulary Building

Exercise A: Choose the option (**a**, **b**, **c** or **d**) which fits best each sentence.

1. He had no formal ………. as a clerk.
   a. study
   b. stretch
   c. training
   d. course

2. He has now become a ………. officer in the army.
   a. significant
   b. superior
   c. enhanced
   d. social

Exercise B: Fill in the blanks in the following sentences using the correct form of the words from the box below. There are 2 extra words in the box you do not need to use.

a. demonstrate	b. augment	c. perform	d. receive	e. illustrate

1. The students …… performed …… really well on their exams last semester.
2. …… Augmenting …… her income was her main concern now that she was divorced.
3. I am sure that you will be …… receiving …… a good report of the group's activities.

Exercise C: Fill in the definitions using words from the box below. There are 2 extra words in the box that you do not need to use.

a. increase	b. intelligence	c. behavior	d. ability	e. point

1. …… Point …… is a single unit in measuring.
2. …… Intelligence …… refers to the faculty of thought and reason.
3. …… Increase …… means growth in size or quantity.

Exercise D: Fill in the chart with the derivatives of the given adjectives or adverbs. Then, provide one **synonym** and one **antonym**, taking into account their meaning in the specific text above.

	Verb	Noun	Adjective	Adverb
1.	signify	significance	significant	significantly
2.	socialize	socialization	social	socially
3.	similize	similarity	similar	similarly
4.	specify	specification	specific	specifically

		Synonym	Antonym
1.	significant	important/striking	unimportant/insignificant
2.	social	communal/societal	private/asocial
3.	similar	analogous/corresponding	different/dissimilar
4.	specifically	especially	generally

Exercise E: Write 4 sentences using the following words: unimportant, generally, private, dissimilar. You must write 1 sentence for each of these words. Use between 8 and 15 words in each sentence. (Suggested Answers)

1. I will not waste any more time on unimportant matters.
2. Generally speaking, I am satisfied with your performance.
3. He did not wish to make his private life public.
4. If you examine the two artists, you'll see their styles aren't so dissimilar.

Music Education

Paragraph 3

Music education has also **demonstrated** the ability to augment a student's IQ. **A** Studies have illustrated significant increases in the IQ of children who have music education versus those that don't. **B** Students in the study who took weekly voice and piano lessons for a nine-month stretch performed better on intelligence tests than those that didn't receive such music education, where their IQs were tested before and after the training. **C** Specifically, the students who received music classes tested three points higher than those who didn't take the classes. Furthermore, these students demonstrated superior social behavior skills than those that didn't take such courses. **D** Students who also took drama and theater classes during this stretch demonstrated similar enhanced IQ and skill sets.

Reading Comprehension

1. The word **demonstrated** in §3 is closest in meaning to
   a. debunked.
   b. stressed.
   c. showed.
   d. disproved.

2. According to the passage, what is the relationship between IQ and fine arts education?
   a. Music education has no impact on the IQ of a student.
   b. Music classes have proved to enhance the IQ of children.
   c. Music classes are less effective than computer classes for a child's IQ.
   d. Studies are inconclusive when measuring music and its impact on IQ.

3. Why does the author mention the effects of drama courses on IQ test performance?
   a. to discredit his argument on the benefits of music education
   b. to show further how fine arts education benefits child development
   c. to contradict those that think music is a beneficial resource for child growth
   d. to make the case that drama classes are more important than music courses

4. Which sentence below best expresses the essential information in the underlined sentence in §3?
   a. Studying music only benefits a child in their ability to take tests.
   b. Studying music improves both the academic and social abilities of children.
   c. Studying drama proves more effective in social development than music education.
   d. Studying drama has little impact on the IQ test performance of young children.

5. All of the following describe the relationship between IQ and arts education **EXCEPT**
   a. higher test scores.
   b. higher drop-out rates.
   c. enhanced social skills.
   d. mental versatility.

6. Look at the four squares, **A**, **B**, **C** and **D**, which indicate where the following sentence could be added to the passage. Where would the sentence best fit?

Right Answer: D

These enhanced skills enabled them to negotiate life circumstances and people, thereby giving them an advantage over others.

7. An introductory sentence for a brief summary of the passage is provided below. Complete the summary by selecting the **THREE** answer choices that express the most important ideas in the passage. Some sentences do not belong in the summary because they express ideas that are not presented in the passage or are ideas of minor importance. **This question is worth 2 points.**

Fine arts education bolsters the IQ development of children who are exposed to the discipline.

a. Studying drama hurts a student's ability to manage social situations.
b. Music education helps children to score higher on standardized tests.
c. Exposure to the fine arts has done little to make children better at life.
d. Social skills become more refined with exposure to music, art and theater.
e. Institutional research has documented benefits in IQ development stemming from fine arts education.

Music Education

Paragraph 4

Studies have also found that the brain of a child who studies music works differently than that of a student not **exposed** to music. Children who receive music education **experience** higher **growth rates** of **neural function** than those who don't. In other words, playing an **instrument essentially requires** a person to use more of their brain, thereby enabling a person to develop parts of it that traditionally would go **undeveloped** without it. Indeed, studies at a **research institute** in Boston have shown that children who study music have enhanced **capacities** to **distinguish** between sounds and **negotiate** motor tasks more seamlessly. Studying music, brain scans illustrated, made **networks** in the human brain **dedicated** to those types of tasks more refined. So, these children were **provided** with an **advantage** in the classroom over their **contemporaries**.

Vocabulary Building

Exercise A: Choose the option (**a**, **b**, **c** or **d**) which fits best each sentence.

1. The ………. of the brake is to stop the car.

a. growth   c. capacity

b. function   d. advantage

2. She's very ………. to her studies.

a. neural   c. dedicated

b. refined   d. undeveloped

Exercise B: Fill in the blanks in the following sentences using the correct form of the words from the box below. There are 2 extra words in the box you do not need to use.

a. expose	b. experience	c. require	d. distinguish	e. provide	f. negotiate

1. She …… negotiated …… a difficult music passage at last night's concert.
2. …… Distinguishing …… between right and wrong is not always easy.
3. The troops were …… exposed …… to gunfire during the battle.
4. It was a difficult time when he …… experienced …… the trauma of his parents' divorce.

Exercise C: Fill in the definitions using words from the box below. There are 2 extra words in the box that you do not need to use.

a. rate	b. instrument	c. institute	d. network	e. contemporary	f. research

1. …… Network …… is a complex and interconnected system.
2. …… Rate …… means a measure of the frequency of occurrence of a given event.
3. …… Contemporary …… is a person of the same age or time.
4. …… Institute …… refers to an organization founded for a specific cause.

Exercise D: Fill in the chart with the derivatives of the given adjectives or adverbs. Then, provide one **synonym** and one **antonym**, taking into account their meaning in the specific text above.

	Verb	Noun	Adjective	Adverb
1.	refine	refinement/refinery	refined	refinedly
2.	dedicate	dedication	dedicated	dedicatedly
3.	develop	development	undeveloped	-
4.	-	essential/essentiality	essential	essentially

		Synonym	Antonym
1.	refined	subtle/sophisticated	unsophisticated
2.	dedicated	devoted/assigned	irrelevant
3.	undeveloped	unexploited	developed
4.	essentially	fundamentally	unnecessarily

Exercise E: Write 4 sentences using the following words: developed, unnecessarily, irrelevant, unsophisticated. You must write 1 sentence for each of these words. Use between 8 and 15 words in each sentence.

(Suggested Answers)

1. Traveling to some less developed areas of the world was a great experience.
2. I really don't want him to suffer unnecessarily.
3. Can we please avoid irrelevant comments in this discussion?
4. How can you accept such an unsophisticated approach?

Debate I

Music Education

Paragraph 4

A Studies have also found that the brain of a child who studies music works differently than that of a student not exposed to music. B Children who receive music education experience higher growth rates of neural function than those who don't. C In other words, playing an instrument **essentially** requires a person to use more of their brain, thereby enabling a person to develop parts of it that traditionally would go undeveloped without it. Indeed, studies at a research institute in Boston have shown that children who study music have enhanced capacities to distinguish between sounds and negotiate motor tasks more seamlessly. D Studying music, brain scans illustrated, made networks in the human brain dedicated to those types of tasks more refined. So, these children were provided with an advantage in the classroom over their contemporaries.

Reading Comprehension

1. The word **essentially** in §4 is closest in meaning to
   a. equally.
   b. basically.
   c. unimportantly.
   d. relatively.

2. Based on the passage, what is the difference between students who do and don't study music?
   a. Music education results in weaker brain development.
   b. Music education hurts larger neural growth.
   c. Music education increases neural activity and growth.
   d. Music education holds back larger brain activity and development.

3. Why does the author refer to a specific research conclusion?
   a. to underscore how the brain positively responds to fine arts education
   b. to contradict evidence of music improving motor skills
   c. to support the argument for more science-based learning in schools
   d. to illustrate how the mind shrivels with exposure to music and art

4. Which sentence below best expresses the essential information in the underlined sentence in §4?
   a. Brain function and activity falls with increased exposure to fine arts training.
   b. The mind becomes less nimble with music education.
   c. Fine arts education enhances the power of the mind to function.
   d. Exposure to music lowers neural activity in a child's brain.

5. All of the following were findings from the Boston institute study on music education **EXCEPT**
   a. motor skills were weakened.
   b. neural activity was increased.
   c. sound recognition was improved.
   d. use of the brain was enhanced.

6. Look at the four squares, A , B , C and D , which indicate where the following sentence could be added to the passage. Where would the sentence best fit?   Right Answer: C

   Playing an instrument strengthens the size and capacity of a child's brain.

7. Select the appropriate sentences from the answer choices and match them to the relationship between brain development and music education. **TWO** of the answer choices will **NOT** be used. **This question is worth 3 points.**

   a. The brain developed more fully and powerfully.
   b. Children possessed enhanced motor skills.
   c. Brain scans produced little insight into mind development.
   d. Children find it more difficult to complete motor tasks.
   e. Students failed to develop full potential of their minds.
   f. Brain imaging showed an inability to learn.
   g. Children were able to identify sounds more easily.

Recipient of Music Education:	A/B/G
Non-Recipient of Music Education:	D/E

Music Education

Paragraph 5

A **similar** study at a **university** in California also **concluded** that students who received some **form** of musical education had enhanced **development** of their **spatial** intelligence. In other words, exposure to music helped these kids to better **interpret factors** that **complement** one another. This skill is often **employed** in **subjects** such as math and science, where students are required to use this type of logic and **reasoning** to solve **posed** problems. More **specifically**, the researchers behind the study concluded that music helped **nurture** these skills that are used in **challenges** found in the **fields** of architecture, art, engineering and computer science. **Ironically**, perhaps, exposure to this **humanity assisted** students in becoming better at subjects **traditionally** thought of as **completely separate** from music education.

Vocabulary Building

Exercise A: Choose the option (**a**, **b**, **c** or **d**) which fits best each sentence.

1. Physical activity is one of the main …… helping to establish good health.

   a. factors
   b. subjects
   c. fields
   d. forms

2. ……….. we eat turkey at Thanksgiving.

   a. Traditionally
   b. Ironically
   c. Completely
   d. Specifically

Exercise B: Fill in the blanks in the following sentences using words from the box. You may need to change the word. There are 2 extra words in the box you do not need to use.

a. conclude	b. interpret	c. complement	d. employ	e. nurture	f. assist

1. Good wine always …… complements …… a good meal.
2. Mary's interest in literature was …… nurtured …… by her parents.
3. He …… interpreted …… her smile as an agreement.
4. Is another salesperson …… assisting …… you or may I help you?

Exercise C: Fill in the definitions using words from the box below. There are 2 extra words in the box that you do not need to use.

a. university	b. development	c. reasoning	d. challenge	e. humanity	f. form

1. …… Challenge …… means a test of someone's abilities.
2. …… Humanity …… refers to the study of literature, philosophy or the arts.
3. …… Reasoning …… is the capacity to make inferences, conclusions etc.
4. …… University …… is an institution for higher level learning.

Exercise D: Fill in the chart with the derivatives of the given adjectives or adverbs. Then, provide one **synonym** and one **antonym**, taking into account their meaning in the specific text above.

	Verb	Noun	Adjective	Adverb
1.	separate	separateness	separate	separately
2.	specify	specification	specific	specifically
3.	-	irony	ironic/ironical	ironically
4.	complete	completion	complete	completely

		Synonym	Antonym
1.	separate	independent/irrelevant	unconnected/interdependent
2.	specifically	particularly	generally
3.	ironically	paradoxically	logically/rationally
4.	completely	totally/entirely	relatively/slightly

Exercise E: Write 4 sentences using the following words: relatively, generally, rationally, interdependent. You must write 1 sentence for each of these words. Use between 8 and 15 words in each sentence.(Suggested Answers)

1. I think that this is a relatively minor problem compared to all others.
2. The child generally had little to say in his defense.
3. They managed to act rationally despite the fear of others.
4. Today, we have to recognize that countries can only be interdependent.

Debate I

Music Education

Paragraph 5

A A similar study at a university in California, also concluded that students who received some form of musical education had enhanced development of their spatial intelligence. **B** In other words, exposure to music helped these kids to better interpret factors that complement one another. **C** This skill is often employed in subjects such as math and science, where students are required to use this type of logic and reasoning to solve posed problems. More specifically, the researchers behind the study concluded that music helped **nurture** these skills that are used in challenges found in the fields of architecture, art, engineering and computer science. Ironically, perhaps, exposure to this humanity assisted students in becoming better at subjects traditionally thought of as completely separate from music education. **D**

Reading Comprehension

1. The word **nurture** in §5 is closest in meaning to
   a. neutralize.
   b. erode.
   c. weaken.
   d. develop.

2. Based on the passage, how does music education affect a student's performance in math and science?
   a. Music education helps students to excel in these subjects.
   b. Music curriculum hurts their ability to excel in these fields of study.
   c. Music education has little effect on performance in the sciences.
   d. Music curriculum only helped math students but did little for science students.

3. Why does the author discuss the benefits to spatial intelligence provided by music education?
   a. to show how only engineers benefit from learning music and art in school
   b. to demonstrate how learning music can enhance a student's performance as a writer
   c. to illustrate how music develops skills that are transferable to other disciplines
   d. to debunk the idea that music education has some benefit outside of the classroom

4. Which sentence below best expresses the essential information in the underlined sentence in §5?
   a. Learning music unsurprisingly benefits a student's ability to perform in other subjects.
   b. Studying music helps children perform better in subjects thought to be unrelated to fine arts.
   c. Music curriculum in schools surprisingly has little impact on math and science skills.
   d. Fine arts education should be reevaluated by studies in Boston and California.

5. All of the following describe the relationship between music and spatial intelligence **EXCEPT**
   a. music helps to develop versatile skills.
   b. engineers may benefit from music training.
   c. teachers need to study less music.
   d. students who study music find it easier to make connections between disciplines.

6. Look at the four squares, **A**, **B**, **C** and **D**, which indicate where the following sentence could be added to the passage. Where would the sentence best fit?

   Right Answer: B

   This research project found that exposure to music made it easier for students to make connections between subject matters.

7. Select the appropriate sentences from the answer choices and match them to the relationship between spatial intelligence and music education. **TWO** of the answer choices will **NOT** be used. **This question is worth 3 points.**

   a. Students find it harder to make connections between abstract ideas.
   b. Students fall behind their peers in math and science performance.
   c. Students navigate concepts that seem to be unrelated much easier.
   d. Students perform well in professions that require creative thinking.
   e. Students interested in building may have better conceptual skills by studying the piano.
   f. Students show little interest in learning about the history of world travelers.
   g. Students find it hard to cope in jobs that use three-dimensional thinking.

Recipient of Music Education:	C/D/E
Non-Recipient of Music Education:	A/G

Debate I

Music Education

Paragraph 6

The **benefits** of music education have also been made **evident** in **standardized** test **performance**. A study **published** early this **decade**, **conducted** by researchers at an institute in Michigan, **revealed** that kids who received some **sort** of music education in **elementary** school performed 20 percent better on math and verbal **portions** of standardized tests than those that didn't. These researchers **attributed** the **discipline** and **focus** required to study music as skills that enabled these students to outperform their contemporaries on the tests. The **investigators** argued that, despite the test score **indications**, educational institutions that offer high-quality music education often have **equally capable** teachers for other subjects. They believe that an education environment that nurtures a **community** to do a great deal of **creative** and **smart** things tends to **translate** into overall outperformance of its students across disciplines. Further, music education, they found, enhances a student's ability to **recall** from their memory verbal information.

Vocabulary Building

Exercise A: Choose the option (**a**, **b**, **c** or **d**) which fits best each sentence.

1. He gave no .... that he was ready to compromise.
   a. sort
   b. portion
   c. focus
   d. indication

2. Reluctance was .... in her voice as she accepted the invitation.
   a. evident
   b. smart
   c. elementary
   d. standardized

Exercise B: Fill in the blanks in the following sentences using words from the box. You may need to change the word. There are 2 extra words in the box you do not need to use.

| a. reveal | b. attribute | c. publish | d. recall | e. conduct | f. translate |

1. I often ....recall.......... the time we spent together in Spain.
2. They ....conducted.......... an experiment before they could decide on the course of action.
3. We ....attributed.......... our failure to lack of preparation. We could have been organized better.
4. ....Translating.......... a literary text is not an easy task.

Exercise C: Fill in the definitions using words from the box below. There are 2 extra words in the box that you do not need to use.

| a. benefit | b. performance | c. decade | d. discipline | e. investigator | f. community |

1. ....Decade.......... is a period of ten years.
2. ....Investigator.......... means a scientist who devotes him/herself to research.
3. ....Benefit.......... refers to an advantage; something that enhances well-being.
4. ....Discipline.......... is a branch of knowledge or teaching.

Exercise D: Fill in the chart with the derivatives of the given adjectives or adverbs. Then, provide one **synonym** and one **antonym**, taking into account their meaning in the specific text above.

	Verb	Noun	Adjective	Adverb
1.	standardize	standardization	standardized	-
2.	create	creation	creative	creatively
3.	-	capability/capableness	capable	capably
4.	equal/equalize	equality	equal	equally

		Synonym	Antonym
1.	standardized	regulated/graded	customized/individualized
2.	creative	imaginative	uncreative/unoriginal
3.	capable	competent	incompetent/incapable
4.	equally	similarly	unequally/unevenly

Exercise E: Write 4 sentences using the following words: unevenly, customized, unoriginal, incapable. You must write 1 sentence for each of these words. Use between 8 and 15 words in each sentence.(Suggested Answers)

1. It was not fair that the profits were distributed unevenly.
2. These may be standard forms but can be customized for personal use.
3. The manuscript contained unoriginal pieces, taken from other writers' works.
4. I think he is incapable of understanding the matter.

Music Education

Paragraph 6

The benefits of music education have also been made evident in standardized test performance. **A** A study published early this decade, conducted by researchers at an institute in Michigan, revealed that kids who received some sort of music education in elementary school performed 20 percent better on math and verbal portions of standardized tests than those that didn't. **B** These researchers attributed the discipline and focus required to study music as skills that enabled these students to outperform their contemporaries on the tests. The investigators argued that, despite the test score indications, educational institutions that offer high-quality music education often have equally capable teachers for other subjects. **C** They believe that an education environment that nurtures a community to do a great deal of creative and smart things tends to translate into overall outperformance of its students across disciplines. Further, music education, they found, enhances a student's ability to recall from their memory verbal information. **D**

Reading Comprehension

1. The word **contemporaries** in §6 is closest in meaning to
   a. peers.
   b. enemies.
   c. ancestors.
   d. superiors.

2. According to the passage, why does music help students take tests better?
   a. It makes students less flexible intellectually.
   b. It helps students develop the skills needed to excel in exams.
   c. It helps students to retain information for a shorter period of time.
   d. It makes students more likely to miss connections between subjects.

3. What do the researchers conclude about schools that teach music education?
   a. The quality of their teachers is lacking compared to schools that don't.
   b. They often possess superior teachers in other subject matters as well.
   c. Their teachers lack intellectual creativity and acumen.
   d. These schools need to catch-up to the performance of schools that only teach science and math.

4. Which sentence below best expresses the essential information in the underlined sentence in §6?
   a. There is no relationship between the culture of a school and the performance of its students.
   b. Schools that encourage initiative and innovation tend to see results in every measure.
   c. Schools that stress math and science perform better than those schools that don't.
   d. Schools that develop well-rounded teachers tend to produce one-dimensional students.

5. All of the following are benefits of studying music **EXCEPT**
   a. better concentration.
   b. shorter recall.
   c. longer focus.
   d. mediocre communication skills.

6. Look at the four squares, **A**, **B**, **C** and **D**, which indicate where the following sentence could be added to the passage. Where would the sentence best fit?

   Right Answer: D

   Ultimately, this may only be the beginning of what researchers discover in terms of music education and its benefits.

7. Select the appropriate sentences from the answer choices and match them to the relationship between music education and standardized testing. **TWO** of the answer choices will **NOT** be used. **This question is worth 3 points.**

   a. Students achieved higher results in math only.
   b. Students experienced better performance in verbal testing.
   c. Students had better recall in communication.
   d. Students had weaker math skills than engineering students.
   e. Students were deficient in the habits associated with outperformance.
   f. Students' memory skills were of a lower caliber.
   g. Students struggled to score higher on math and verbal testing.

Recipient of Music Education:	B/C
Non-Recipient of Music Education:	E/F/G

Music Education

Paragraph 7

Though music education has demonstrated benefits in **improving** the **overall academic** and social performance of students, **experts caution parents** not to **overestimate** music education. Exposure to music alone does not make a child smarter. Rather, parents should **provide** musical training to their children more out of a desire to make them **appreciate** the art form and its **affiliated** disciplines, including singing, playing an instrument and reading music. **Developing skills** in these areas have their own **value** outside of any **secondary** benefits. Studying music provides an **ideal opportunity** for children to **understand culture** and even themselves a bit better, whereby students form a **broader viewpoint** of the world where they are **able** to **express** and feel things that **enrich** their lives as human beings.

Vocabulary Building

Exercise A: Choose the option (**a**, **b**, **c** or **d**) which fits best each sentence.

1. I really ………. your help on the matter.

   a. overestimate   **c.** express

   b. appreciate   **d.** understand

2. You can use the Internet as a(n) ………. source of information.

   a. overall   **c. secondary**

   b. affiliated   **d.** broad

Exercise B: Fill in the blanks in the following sentences using words from the box. You may need to change the word. There are 2 extra words in the box you do not need to use.

a. improve	b. caution	c. provide	d. develop	e. appreciate	f. enrich

1. I greatly …… enriched …… my experiences as I was traveling around the world.
2. Our boss always …… cautions …… us against exceeding optimism.
3. We should …… provide …… food and shelter for the homeless.
4. …… Improving …… the working conditions is our main concern.

Exercise C: Fill in the definitions using words from the box below. There are 2 extra words in the box that you do not need to use.

a. expert	b. parent	c. skill	d. value	e. opportunity	f. viewpoint

1. …… Viewpoint …… is a mental position from which things are seen.
2. …… Value …… refers to worth in usefulness or importance.
3. …… Opportunity …… means a chance or prospect.
4. …… Skill …… is a developed talent or ability.

Exercise D: Fill in the chart with the derivatives of the given adjectives or adverbs. Then, provide one **synonym** and one **antonym**, taking into account their meaning in the specific text above.

	Verb	Noun	Adjective	Adverb
1.	affiliate	affiliation	affiliated	-
2.	broaden	breadth	broad	broadly
3.	idealize	idealization	ideal	ideally
4.	enable	ability	able	ably

		Synonym	Antonym
1.	affiliated	associated/connected	separated/unrelated
2.	broad	wide/far-reaching	narrow/limited
3.	ideal	perfect/optimal	unsuitable/imperfect
4.	able	capable/competent	incapable/incompetent

Exercise E: Write 4 sentences using the following words: narrow, unsuitable, incompetent, unrelated. You must write 1 sentence for each of these words. Use between 8 and 15 words in each sentence. (Suggested Answers)

1. I'm afraid we are working on very narrow resources.
2. I'm sorry Miss but this is unsuitable attire for the occasion.
3. Incompetent employees will have to be fired eventually.
4. Both of them died but of totally unrelated causes.

Music Education

Paragraph 7

A Though music education has demonstrated benefits in improving the overall academic and social performance of students, experts caution parents not to **overestimate** music education. **B** Exposure to music alone does not make a child smarter. Rather, parents should provide musical training to their children more out of a desire to make them appreciate the art form and its affiliated disciplines, including singing, playing an instrument and reading music. <u>Developing skills in these areas have their own value outside of any secondary benefits.</u> **C** Studying music provides an ideal opportunity for children to understand culture and even themselves a bit better, whereby students form a broader viewpoint of the world where they are able to express and feel things that enrich their lives as human beings. **D**

Reading Comprehension

1. The word **overestimate** in §7 is closest in meaning to
   a. undervalue.
   b. overemphasize.
   c. overbear.
   d. demystify.

2. Based on the passage, what should be the students' objective for music education?
   a. to develop the skills to score higher on standardized tests
   b. to have something interesting to add to their resume
   c. to learn to enjoy the art form
   d. to discover the relationship between science and art

3. Why do experts warn parents not to place too much importance on music education?
   a. Studying music makes students more intelligent for life.
   b. The focus on it provides little benefit outside of school.
   c. The focus on it should be to develop an understanding of the art form.
   d. Studying music is largely a leisure for only the most wealthy students.

4. Which sentence below best expresses the essential information in the underlined sentence in §7?
   a. Learning music for its own sake provides enough incentive.
   b. Learning music should focus on how it can better performance in math.
   c. Learning music has little impact on college admission and test performance.
   d. Learning music should only be done by someone with a lot of money.

5. All of the following are reasons to pursue a music education **EXCEPT**
   a. cultural awareness.
   b. testing skills.
   c. world understanding.
   d. human experience.

6. Look at the four squares, **A**, **B**, **C** and **D**, which indicate where the following sentence could be added to the passage. Where would the sentence best fit? Right Answer: B

   At times, the academic benefits of the discipline can be exaggerated.

7. Select the appropriate sentences from the answer choices and match them to the motivations for studying music. **TWO** of the answer choices will **NOT** be used. **This question is worth 3 points.**

   a. to develop an appreciation for the art form
   b. to exclusively enhance standardized test performance
   c. to learn how to write operas like Mozart
   d. to discover how the art form can enrich a student's life
   e. to seek benefits in other academic subject matters
   f. to kill time after school when a student is bored
   g. to learn about culture and other parts of the world

Reasons to Study Music:	A/D/G
Reasons not related to Studying Music:	B/E

Debate I

Debate I

Extracurricular Activities

Paragraph 1

My son Matthew, a third grader at the local **elementary** school, **participates** in three **extracurricular** classes per week. On Tuesday, he takes piano lessons with a wonderful teacher who studies at Julliard. After school on Wednesday, we go to his Spanish class with a native speaker from Madrid. And, on Friday after school, he takes vocal lessons with a singing teacher that sang back-up for Bruce Springsteen. The Spanish class, my husband and I believe, should **serve** him well considering the **growth** of Spanish-speakers in our native city of Los Angeles. The other two classes, however, don't hold much value in today's world.

Paragraph 2

Don't get me wrong, this doesn't mean that these **seemingly** valueless activities are a bad way for our son to spend his time. There are many things one does in life that don't have some deep meaning or long-term value. Hobbies, for most people, are there simply to **pass** the time, rather than provide some deep **sense** of **purpose** or **enrichment**. Matthew looks forward to his piano and vocal classes to see his teachers and improve his skill set. He seems to be **content** with that **measurement** for it and so am I.

Paragraph 3

Some parents, though, are not content with such **superficial evaluation** of these activities. They **operate** with the belief that music and performing arts education are **vital** for their child's development and that these class-es provide them with an **advantage** in school and in life. I couldn't **disagree** more. Indeed, the classes are great, and I'm all for **public** schools having to offer music, art and other related classes, **especially** in commu-nities where parents don't have the **discretionary income** to pay for **private** classes. But I don't think that a student is really any better off in the long run for having studied ballet or the violin than a child who has not **undertaken** the discipline. Of course, if no one ever chose to study a classical music instrument, we wouldn't have professional institutions for all to enjoy, which would **detract** from our society. But it is not necessary for every child to study these art forms.

Paragraph 4

Don't get me wrong, these classes are not a waste of time entirely**.** There are benefits to studying the perform-ing arts in terms of **instilling** values of **patience** and **discipline**. At the same time, these **traits** can also be learned by playing sports or taking an after school job. I don't think there are any **unique** values to knowing how to play the cello, versus playing baseball, unless you are **particularly** talented at playing the instrument. If not, then, I think, a child can **acquire** the same skills by practicing **martial** arts or tennis.

Paragraph 5

Of course, we can all agree that it's important for children to be **exposed** to a variety of activities and hobbies to see what they enjoy and are good at **accomplishing**. However, I don't think that the value of what they choose to practice should be **judged** strictly for some **perceived** long-term benefit. I believe, regardless of the skills acquired or not, kids should participate in activities that they may take with them later into life. I'd rather my son became a **culinary enthusiast** young in life and keep it with him simply because he enjoys it, not necessarily because he **envisions** a career as a chef or because a research study finds that cooking improves a student's ability to score **perfectly** on a standardized test.

Paragraph 6

For now, Matthew will continue with his weekly **regimen** of activities. I ask him from time to time if he still enjoys the classes and, so far, he says yes. If he changes his mind at some **point** to take up tennis or simply wants to take a break from it all and be a kid, I won't **mind.** I want my son to enjoy being a child and to have some space for his **tastes** to change and his **curiosity** to grow. I see no value in having an over-programmed child **rushing** from class-to-class because some researcher thinks it will be the difference between success and failure in life. I'll take my chances with letting him just be my son.

Vocabulary Building

Exercise A: Choose the option (**a**, **b**, **c** or **d**) which fits best each sentence.

1. If we work all together, we can .... our goal.
   a. participate
   b. operate
   c. undertake
   d. accomplish

2. We are working toward the .... of the students' reading skills.
   a. growth
   b. purpose
   c. enrichment
   d. advantage

3. I had to make only some .... changes in our program.
   a. content
   b. superficial
   c. discretionary
   d. unique

4. .... is the final component of this training course.
   a. Measurement
   b. Evaluation
   c. Discipline
   d. Sense

5. He failed to .... the true nature of their relationship.
   a. perceive
   b. envision
   c. mind
   d. judge

6. Sports is the most popular .... activity.
   a. elementary
   b. extracurricular
   c. culinary
   d. martial

Exercise B: Fill in the blanks in the following sentences using words from the box. You may need to change the word. There are 2 extra words in the box you do not need to use.

a. serve	b. pass	c. disagree	d. detract	e. instill	f. acquire	g. expose	h. rush

1. Her presence ......instilled...... faith into the children who were almost desperate.
2. Our goal is to ......expose...... our children to classical music.
3. The sample was representative, ...serving...... the purposes of our research.
4. He ......rushed...... out of his office just a minute ago.
5. The days were ......passing...... slowly in the quiet country house.
6. This change in the initial testimony ......detracts...... from the strength of your case.

Exercise C: Fill in the definitions using words from the box below. There are 2 extra words in the box that you do not need to use.

a. income	b. patience	c. trait	d. enthusiast	e. regimen	f. point	g. taste	h. curiosity

1. ......Regimen...... is a regulated system that may promote a beneficiary effect.
2. ......Income...... means the amount of money gained through work; salary.
3. ......Trait...... means a distinguishing feature; a person's quality.
4. ......Curiosity...... is a desire to know and learn about people or things.
5. ......Patience...... means the ability to calmly undergo difficult experiences.
6. ......Taste...... is a personal preference or liking.

Exercise D: Fill in the chart with the derivatives of the given adjectives or adverbs. Then, provide one **synonym** and one **antonym**, taking into account their meaning in the specific text above.

	Verb	Noun	Adjective	Adverb			Synonym	Antonym
1.	vitalize	vitality	vital	vitally	1.	vital	fundamental/critical	trivial/minor
2.	specialize	specialty	special	especially	2.	especially	specifically/mostly	generally/broadly
3.	publicize	publication/publisher	public	publically	3.	public	state/free	nonpublic/private
4.	privatize	privacy/privatization	private	privately	4.	private	nonpublic/exclusive	public/state
5.	particularize	particular	particular	particularly	5.	particularly	notably/exceptionally	normally/commonly
6.	perfect	perfection	perfect	perfectly	6.	perfectly	flawlessly/impeccably	badly/poorly

Exercise E: Write 6 sentences using the following words: commonly, nonpublic, broadly, state, poorly, minor. You must write 1 sentence for each of these words. Use between 8 and 15 words in each sentence. (Suggested Answers)

1. He was commonly known among friends as Big Bob.
2. It is not always a fact that nonpublic schools are better than public ones.
3. He broadly got what he intended to from the meeting.
4. It is one of your legal rights to enroll your child in a state school.
5. He always performed poorly when he was at school.
6. We may need to make some minor changes in the document.

TOEFL Exam Practice: Reading Comprehension

Paragraph 1

My son Matthew, a third grader at the local elementary school, participates in three **enriching** classes per week. On Tuesday, he takes piano lessons with a wonderful teacher who studies at Julliard. After school on Wednesday, we go to his Spanish class with a native speaker from Madrid. And on Friday after school, he takes vocal lessons with a singing teacher that sang back-up for Bruce Springsteen. The Spanish class, my husband and I believe, should serve him well considering the growth of Spanish-speakers in our native city of Los Angeles. The other two classes, however, don't hold much value in today's world.

1. The word **enriching** in §1 is closest in meaning to
   a. supplemental.
   b. ridiculous.
   c. evident.
   d. detracting.

2. Based on the passage, why does the author think his son's Spanish classes are beneficial?
   a. Learning Spanish is required by the child's school to graduate.
   b. There is a growing population that speaks the language.
   c. Foreign language skills are a requirement for college admission.
   d. Spanish-speakers are becoming less of the population demographics.

Paragraph 2

Don't get me wrong, this doesn't mean that these **seemingly** valueless activities are a bad way for our son to spend his time. There are many things one does in life that don't have some deep meaning or long-term value. Hobbies, for most people, are there simply to pass the time, rather than provide some deep sense of purpose or enrichment. Matthew looks forward to his piano and vocal classes to see his teachers and improve his skill set. He seems to be content with that measurement for it and so am I.

3. The phrase **don't get me wrong** in §2 is closest in meaning to
   a. do not comprehend.   c. do not believe.
   b. do not misunderstand.   d. do not meander.

4. The word **seemingly** in §2 is closest in meaning to
   a. exterior.   c. at last glance.
   b. on the surface.   d. exceedingly.

5. Why does the author mention his son's attitude toward his extracurricular activities?
   a. to illustrate that his son dislikes them
   b. to show how the parent is always in charge
   c. to establish his son's expectations for them
   d. to confuse the reader with his intent

Paragraph 3

Some parents, though, are not content with such superficial evaluation of these activities. They operate with the belief that music and performing arts education are vital for their child's development and that these classes provide them with an advantage in school and in life. I couldn't disagree more. Indeed, the classes are great, and I'm all for public schools having to offer music, art and other related classes, especially in communities where parents don't have the discretionary income to pay for private classes. But I don't think that a student is really any better off in the long run for having studied ballet or the violin than a child who has not **undertaken** the discipline. Of course, if no one ever chose to study a classical music instrument, we wouldn't have professional institutions for all to enjoy, which would detract from our society. But it is not necessary for every child to study these art forms.

6. What does the author disagree with concerning performing arts classes?
   a. These classes serve no real value.
   b. These classes are necessary for a child's full development.
   c. These classes are becoming obsolete as the digital economy progresses.
   d. These classes have become too costly for schools to afford.

7. The word **undertaken** in §3 is closest in meaning to
   a. finished.
   b. experienced.
   c. walked away from.
   d. underestimated.

Paragraph 4

Don't get me wrong, these classes are not a waste of time entirely. There are benefits to studying the performing arts in terms of **instilling** values of patience and discipline. At the same time, these traits can also be learned by playing sports or taking an after school job. I don't think there are any unique values to knowing how to play the cello, versus playing baseball, unless you are particularly talented at playing the instrument. If not, then, I think, a child can acquire the same skills by practicing martial arts or tennis.

8. The word **instilling** in §4 is closest in meaning to
   a. nurturing.
   b. burying.
   c. interning.
   d. recalling.

9. According to §4, developing skills like focus and commitment are
   a. completely unique to studying music.
   b. only developed by playing sports.
   c. essentially attainable through a variety of activities.
   d. increasingly more rare in the technological era.

Paragraph 5

Of course, **we can all agree** that it's important for children to be exposed to a variety of activities and hobbies to see what they enjoy and are good at accomplishing. However, I don't think that the value of what they choose to practice should be judged strictly for some perceived long-term benefit. I believe, regardless of the skills acquired or not, kids should participate in activities that they may take with them later into life. I'd rather my son became a culinary enthusiast young in life and keep it with him simply because he enjoys it, not necessarily because he envisions a career as a chef or because a research study finds that cooking improves a student's ability to score perfectly on a standardized test.

10. The phrase **we can all agree** in §5 is closest in meaning to
    a. a general consensus fell through.
    b. a dominant thought exists.
    c. few people see the reality of a situation.
    d. there is discord concerning an idea.

11. All of the following are reasons why the writer's child should pursue an activity **EXCEPT**
    a. pleasure.
    b. natural interest.
    c. test performance.
    d. life-long hobby.

12. It can be inferred from §5 that the author
    a. disagrees with his child's motives for learning to cook.
    b. believes that performance on tests should motivate all life decisions.
    c. wants his son to become a chef because of the job prospects.
    d. has a flexible and open approach with raising his son.

Paragraph 6

A For now, Matthew will continue with his weekly regimen of activities. B I ask him from time to time if he still enjoys the classes, and, so far, he says yes. If he changes his mind at some point, to take up tennis or simply wants to take a break from it all and be a kid, I won't mind. I want my son to enjoy being a child and to have some space for his tastes to change and his curiosity to grow. C I see no value in having an over-programmed child rushing from class-to-class because some researcher thinks it will be the difference between success and failure in life. I'll take my chances with letting him just be my son. D

13. Why does the author provide his son with autonomy in deciding which activities he will do?
    a. He wants to control his son at all costs.
    b. He wants his son to develop his own interests and judgment.
    c. He wants his son to become dependent on his father.
    d. He wants his son to prepare for academics exclusively.

14. Look at the four squares, A, B, C and D, which indicate where the following sentence could be added to the passage. Where would the sentence best fit?   Right Answer: C

    Of course, I know that this runs counter to the dominant trends in our culture that stress practicality to a fault, in my opinion.

Paragraphs 1 to 6

15. An introductory sentence for a brief summary of the passage is provided below. Complete the summary by selecting the **THREE** answer choices that express the most important ideas in the passage. Some sentences do not belong in the summary because they express ideas that are not presented in the passage or are ideas of minor importance. **This question is worth 2 points.**

    Stressing education in the arts for practical reasons only undermines the very reason to study them in the first place.

    a. Children should be given space for their curiosity to grow and their interests to change.
    b. It makes a lot of sense to study music or art even without a practical motivation behind it.
    c. Our society needs to use more imagination and flexibility in our educational approaches.
    d. Kids must be empowered to develop their own thinking and let their creativity flourish.
    e. Parents should encourage their children to study the arts to improve their test-taking skills.

Standardized Tests in School

Paragraph 1

With the beginning of each school year, students and teachers **prepare** themselves for taking a **bevy** of standardized tests designed to **determine** their **advancement**, the skills of the teacher, the success of the school and the **capacity** of the student to advance to the next level of education. Not everyone, though, is **contented** with this **approach** to education, as a group of educational **activists**, concerned parents and educators have organized a series of **protests** to **challenge** the test culture that has taken over the **educational landscape**, as they believe the emphasis on testing is hurting children. One **advocate** against these tests, John Wilson, **founder** of **Citizens** Against Tests, who is a former teacher himself in the New York Public School System, argues that **efforts** of **civil disobedience** are tantamount to change. He believes that the emphasis on testing is part of a larger effort to **undermine** the existing public school system. His organization is **encouraging** parents and students not to take their state's standardized examinations with an **aim** to alter the **premise surrounding** testing as the only way to evaluate students and repair **struggling** schools.

Vocabulary Building

Exercise A: Choose the option (**a**, **b**, **c** or **d**) which fits best each sentence.

1. He is known as a passionate .... of civil rights.

   a. advocate   **c.** citizen
   b. founder   **d.** protest

2. He congratulated them on their .... in the field of medicine.

   a. advancement   **c.** bevy
   b. approach   **d.** capacity

Exercise B: Fill in the blanks in the following sentences using words from the box below. There are 2 extra words in the box you do not need to use. You cannot change the words.

a. prepare	**b.** determine	**c.** challenge	**d.** encourage	**e.** undermine	**f.** surround

1. Fans always ..... surround ..... this singer wherever he goes.
2. I'm afraid that this will ..... undermine ... their chances of success.
3. The committee is going to .... determine ..... the policy we will follow.
4. This was a book that would greatly ..... challenge ..... the beliefs of its time.

Exercise C: Fill in the definitions using words from the box below. There are 2 extra words in the box that you do not need to use.

a. protest	**b.** landscape	**c.** effort	**d.** disobedience	**e.** aim	**f.** premise

1. .... Disobedience ... means refusal to comply or obey.
2. ..... Premise ...... refers to logic; a proposition that helps to support a conclusion.
3. ..... Protest .... is an individual or collective display of disapproval.
4. .... Landscape .... refers to an intellectual field of activity, seen as a whole.

Exercise D: Fill in the chart with the derivatives of the given adjectives or adverbs. Then, provide one **synonym** and one **antonym**, taking into account their meaning in the specific text above.

	Verb	Noun	Adjective	Adverb
1.	content	contentedness	contented	contentedly
2.	civilize	civility/civilization	civil	civilly
3.	educate	education/educator	educational	educationally
4.	struggle	struggle	struggling	strugglingly

		Synonym	Antonym
1.	contented	satisfied/pleased	discontented/dissatisfied
2.	civil	civic/civilian	state
3.	educational	school/pedagogic	non-educational
4.	struggling	troubled/agonizing	untroubled

Exercise E: Write 4 sentences using the following words: non-educational, state, dissatisfied, untroubled. You must write 1 sentence for each of these words. Use between 8 and 15 words in each sentence. (Suggested Answers)

1. Engaging in non-educational activities is not a waste of time.
2. Citizens should have a say on matters of the state.
3. I am greatly dissatisfied with his performance.
4. Finally, I can have some untroubled sleep at night.

Standardized Tests in School

Paragraph 1

A With the beginning of each school year, students and teachers prepare themselves for taking a bevy of standardized tests designed to determine their advancement, the skills of the teacher, the success of the school and the capacity of the student to advance to the next level of education. B Not everyone, though, is contented with this approach to education, as a group of educational activists, concerned parents and educators have organized a series of protests to challenge the test culture that has taken over the educational landscape, as they believe the emphasis on testing is hurting children. One advocate against these tests, John Wilson, founder of Citizens Against Tests, who is a former teacher himself in the New York Public School System, argues that efforts of civil disobedience are **tantamount** to change. C He believes that the emphasis on testing is part of a larger effort to undermine the existing public school system. His organization is encouraging parents and students not to take their state's standardized examinations with an aim to alter the premise surrounding testing as the only way to evaluate students and repair struggling schools. D

Reading Comprehension

1. The word **tantamount** in §1 is closest in meaning to
   a. resistant.
   b. insignificant.
   c. optional.
   d. equivalent.

2. Based on the text, why are some people protesting against the use of standardized tests in school?
   a. They enhance student performance in college.
   b. They are taking away from the overall development of children.
   c. They are making the teachers' union stronger.
   d. They have the unquestioned support of parents who want more testing.

3. Why have the protestors chosen forms of civil disobedience to express their views?
   a. It is violent and intimidates people.
   b. It has historically little impact socially.
   c. It is effective in peacefully forging change.
   d. It has alienated teachers from public schools.

4. Which sentence below best expresses the essential information in the underlined sentence in §1?
   a. By not taking the tests, parents will have little impact on changing the testing culture.
   b. By taking the tests, students will improve their chances of getting into better schools.
   c. By taking the tests, parents will make it easier for their voice to be heard on standardized testing.
   d. By not taking the tests, those against them will have leverage to change the testing culture.

5. All of the following have been evaluated through standardized tests **EXCEPT**
   a. teacher performance.
   b. student progress.
   c. parenting skills.
   d. excellence of a school.

6. Look at the four squares, A, B, C and D, which indicate where the following sentence could be added to the passage. Where would the sentence best fit?   Right Answer: B

   Advocates of the testing culture have found tests useful in evaluation and want to develop more examinations as the educational system evolves.

7. An introductory sentence for a brief summary of the passage is provided below. Complete the summary by selecting the **THREE** answer choices that express the most important ideas in the passage. Some sentences do not belong in the summary because they express ideas that are not presented in the passage or are ideas of minor importance. **This question is worth 2 points.**

   The increasing use of standardized testing in schools has raised debate among educational experts.

   a. Standardized tests have a role in measuring student and school performance.
   b. Parents believe these tests have no impact on the development of their children.
   c. Experts question whether too much emphasis has been placed on examinations of this nature.
   d. Ulterior motives may exist for stressing these tests such as changing the public school model.
   e. Teachers disagree with parents regarding the importance of standardized tests.

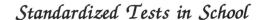

Standardized Tests in School

Paragraph 2
The activists have used a variety of **tactics** to call **attention** to their **cause** including rallies, **direct** mail campaigns and teach-ins to **communicate** to **local** and **federal** educational **bodies** their **sentiment** against educational **reform** that focuses on **corporate** solutions, including **privatization** of schools and **exhaustive** testing. One educational expert, Jane Smith, who has been fighting the **emerging dominance** of standardized testing, believes that more parents are becoming aware of the problems with **excessive** testing and are becoming **increasingly** angry about it. She and the other protestors are **banking** on the fact that if enough students **elect** not to take the examinations the date will become statistically **eroded** and thus invalid, thereby forcing school systems to **negotiate** with organizations like theirs. Of course, the **efficacy** of civil disobedience efforts like this requires tremendous **participation** or it fails. Moreover, even if students choose not to take the tests, they are stuck with an educational approach that is **geared** toward test-taking.

Vocabulary Building

Exercise A: Choose the option (**a**, **b**, **c** or **d**) which fits best each sentence.

1. They're unpopular for their .... over the community.
   a. efficacy
   b. reform
   c. dominance
   d. attention

2. He works in a(n) .... company in South America.
   a. federal
   b. corporate
   c. emerging
   d. excessive

Exercise B: Fill in the blanks in the following sentences using words from the box below. There are 2 extra words in the box you do not need to use. You cannot change the words.

| **a.** communicate | **b.** bank | **c.** elect | **d.** erode | **e.** negotiate | **f.** gear |

1. He will .... gear .... his speech toward a more conservative audience.
2. We should ...... negotiate ..... more as far as the deal is concerned.
3. I cannot .... elect ...... any more classes; I have reached the limit.
4. I'm afraid that jealousy is going to .... erode .... their relationship.

Exercise C: Fill in the definitions using words from the box below. There are 2 extra words in the box that you do not need to use.

| **a.** tactics | **b.** cause | **c.** body | **d.** sentiment | **e.** privatization | **f.** participation |

1. ...... Participation ...... means being involved in the activities of a group.
2. ...... Sentiment ..... is an attitude mainly based on emotion.
3. ...... Tactics ...... refers to a plan for attaining a particular goal.
4. ...... Privatization ... is the process of transferring something from public ownership.

Exercise D: Fill in the chart with the derivatives of the given adjectives or adverbs. Then, provide one **synonym** and one **antonym**, taking into account their meaning in the specific text above.

	Verb	Noun	Adjective	Adverb			Synonym	Antonym
1.	direct	direction	direct	directly	1.	direct	personal/immediate	indirect
2.	localize	local/locality	local	locally	2.	local	regional	national
3.	exhaust	exhaustion	exhausting	exhaustively	3.	exhausting	thorough/detailed	casual/superficial
4.	increase	increase	increasing	increasingly	4.	increasingly	progressively	decreasingly

Exercise E: Write 4 sentences using the following words: national, superficial, indirect, decreasingly. You must write 1 sentence for each of these words. Use between 8 and 15 words in each sentence. (Suggested Answers)

1. Next week there will be the second round of national elections.
2. We had only the time for a superficial analysis of the problem.
3. He made an indirect comment about her appearance.
4. The author's subsequent novels were decreasingly successful.

Standardized Tests in School

Paragraph 2

A The activists have used a variety of tactics to call attention to their cause including rallies, direct mail campaigns and teach-ins to communicate to local and federal educational bodies their sentiment against educational reform that focuses on corporate solutions, including privatization of schools and exhaustive testing. **B** One educational expert, Jane Smith, who has been fighting the **emerging** dominance of standardized testing, believes that more parents are becoming aware of the problems with excessive testing and are becoming increasingly angry about it. **C** She and the other protestors are banking on the fact that if enough students elect not to take the examinations the date will become statistically eroded and thus invalid, thereby forcing school systems to negotiate with organizations like theirs. **D** Of course, the efficacy of civil disobedience efforts like this requires tremendous participation or it fails. <u>Moreover, even if students choose not to take the tests, they are stuck with an educational approach that is geared toward test-taking.</u>

Reading Comprehension

1. The word **emerging** in §2 is closest in meaning to
   a. falling.
   b. intriguing.
   c. arising.
   d. causing.

2. According to the passage, how have parents responded to the testing culture?
   a. They have ignored it largely out of respect for schools.
   b. They have become upset with its consequences for their children.
   c. They have sided with teachers on offering more tests.
   d. They have resisted protesting the trend in schools.

3. Why does the author explore the strategy behind students refusing to take the tests?
   a. to illustrate that they don't care about their education
   b. to show that parents concur with the current testing culture
   c. to illustrate that civil disobedience is ineffective in creating change
   d. to show the relationship between the tactic and the desirable outcome of reducing test emphasis

4. Which sentence below best expresses the essential information in the underlined sentence in §2?
   a. Students who protest the tests will still experience an educational approach focused on standardized tests.
   b. Students who choose to take the tests will have an advantage because of the educational approach aimed at testing.
   c. Students who neglect the tests will have little difficulty learning in the classroom.
   d. Students who sit for the tests will be unprepared to meet the standards for education in the current landscape.

5. Those who oppose the testing culture have used all of the following forms of resistance **EXCEPT**
   a. protests.
   b. mailings.
   c. strikes.
   d. bribery.

6. Look at the four squares, **A**, **B**, **C** and **D**, which indicate where the following sentence could be added to the passage. Where would the sentence best fit?   Right Answer: B

   All of these tactics have created momentum for those looking to change the educational culture.

7. An introductory sentence for a brief summary of the passage is provided below. Complete the summary by selecting the **THREE** answer choices that express the most important ideas in the passage. Some sentences do not belong in the summary because they express ideas that are not presented in the passage or are ideas of minor importance. **This question is worth 2 points.**

   Opposition to the current standardized testing culture has become stronger and more resourceful in advancing their cause.

   a. Organizers have employed a variety of means to express their view and force change to the system.
   b. The debate between the opposition and advocates for testing has reached a consensus on the matter.
   c. Parents have not been moved by the efforts of these groups and increase focus on testing.
   d. By choosing not to take the tests, those who oppose the current system hope to gain power in the debate.
   e. Forms of civil disobedience have impacted the discourse on the testing culture.

Debate 2

Standardized Tests in School

Paragraph 3

It is an **interesting** story of how testing became the **dominant focus** of school systems and thus causes **mass** protests and **demonstrations**. One **former** teacher, Greg Michaels, **cited** testing as the reason he left the **profession**, as he could no longer **bear** having to **devote** so much class time and **preparation** to simply preparing students for one standardized test after another. In his opinion, there is no **dialog** any longer about what **constitutes solid** teaching or **desirable** learning. The **complete** discussion **revolves** around how to raise test scores and how to **leverage** them for more **resources**. Schools, as a result, have become test prep centers rather than places of **broad** learning and development. Gone are the days when students were exposed to art courses, field trips and richer subject matters.

Vocabulary Building

Exercise A: Choose the option (**a**, **b**, **c** or **d**) which fits best each sentence.

1. We can use this evidence as a .... base to rely our research on.
   a. complete   c. mass
   b. broad   **d. solid**

2. He did not even want to see his .... wife.
   a. interesting   c. desirable
   b. dominant   **d. former**

Exercise B: Fill in the blanks in the following sentences using the correct form of the words from the box below. There are 2 extra words in the box you do not need to use.

a. cite	b. bear	c. devote	d. constitute	e. revolve	f. leverage

1. The result hardly ......constitutes...... a victory.
2. She ......cited...... multiple instances of abuse over the years when asked.
3. He ......bore...... all the weight of supporting his family when his father died.
4. ......Devoting...... his free time to his children was his wish.

Exercise C: Fill in the definitions using words from the box below. There are 2 extra words in the box that you do not need to use.

a. demonstration	b. profession	c. dialog	d. resource	e. focus	f. preparation

1. ......Resource...... refers to a source of aid or support.
2. ......Profession...... is an occupation or career.
3. ......Demonstration...... means a public display of a group opinion.
4. ......Focus...... is a center of interest or attention.

Exercise D: Fill in the chart with the derivatives of the given adjectives or adverbs. Then, provide one **synonym** and one **antonym**, taking into account their meaning in the specific text above.

	Verb	Noun	Adjective	Adverb
1.	interest	interest	interesting	interestingly
2.	dominate	dominator/domination	dominant	dominantly
3.	solidify	solidification	solid	solidly
4.	desire	desire	desirable	desirably

		Synonym	Antonym
1.	interesting	fascinating/intriguing	uninteresting/boring
2.	dominant	primary/main	secondary/minor
3.	solid	decent/reliable	unreliable/unsound
4.	desirable	useful/valuable	disadvantageous

Exercise E: Write 4 sentences using the following words: minor, uninteresting, disadvantageous, unsound. You must write 1 sentence for each of these words. Use between 8 and 15 words in each sentence. (Suggested Answers)

1. The building suffered minor damage after the earthquake.
2. The critic claimed the writer's latest work is lifeless and uninteresting.
3. The new government policy has proven to be extremely disadvantageous for us.
4. I'm afraid the conclusion you have drawn is unsound.

Standardized Tests in School

Paragraph 3

It is an interesting story of how testing became the dominant focus of school systems and thus causes mass protests and demonstrations. **A** One former teacher, Greg Michaels, cited testing as the reason he left the profession, as he could no longer bear having to devote so much class time and preparation to simply preparing students for one standardized test after another. **B** In his opinion, there is no dialog any longer about what **constitutes** solid teaching or desirable learning. The complete discussion revolves around how to raise test scores and how to leverage them for more resources. **C** Schools, as a result, have become test prep centers rather than places of broad learning and development. Gone are the days when students were exposed to art courses, field trips and richer subject matters. **D**

Reading Comprehension

1. The word **constitutes** in §3 is closest in meaning to
   a. makes.
   b. detracts.
   c. hurts.
   d. precludes.

2. Based on the text, why have schools placed more emphasis on tests than developing a rich curriculum?
   a. A broad educational approach enables schools to receive more financial backing.
   b. Parents want more testing to measure the achievement of their children.
   c. Higher tests scores translate into more funding for a school.
   d. Students find testing more beneficial to their education than other subjects.

3. Why does the author mention the effects of the testing culture on the educational approach?
   a. to show that standardized examinations have done little to alter past educational models
   b. to show that standardized tests contribute to developing a well-rounded curriculum
   c. to demonstrate how financial incentives have altered the educational landscape
   d. to demonstrate how students respond more positively to a test center school model

4. Which sentence best expresses the essential information in the underlined sentence in §3?
   a. The teacher recommitted to the profession because of the testing culture mandate.
   b. The teacher became alienated from the profession because of the emphasis on teaching.
   c. The teacher changed careers because the testing culture eroded his desire to educate.
   d. The teacher believed that emphasizing tests made his experience as an educator richer.

5. All of the following describe the relationship between testing and education **EXCEPT**
   a. money has influenced the dynamic.
   b. teachers prefer testing over broad education.
   c. what makes good teaching now is no longer examined.
   d. schools have become more of a customer-service business geared toward test preparation.

6. Look at the four squares, **A**, **B**, **C** and **D**, which indicate where the following sentence could be added to the passage. Where would the sentence best fit?

   Right Answer: B

   This experience left him disillusioned with the profession as a whole.

7. An introductory sentence for a brief summary of the passage is provided below. Complete the summary by selecting the **THREE** answer choices that express the most important ideas in the passage. Some sentences do not belong in the summary because they express ideas that are not presented in the passage or are ideas of minor importance. **This question is worth 2 points.**

   The rise of the testing culture has transformed past notions of what education sought to accomplish.

   a. Testing has enriched the overall education of students and teacher satisfaction.
   b. The testing culture has alienated some teachers from the profession.
   c. The emphasis on testing has narrowed the discussion on what makes decent teaching.
   d. Testing has become the preferred method of instruction for experienced teachers.
   e. Standardized testing has narrowed the focus of educational curricula.

Standardized Tests in School

Paragraph 4

Some **blame** this **evolution** on the No Child Left Behind **Act** or Race to the Top Fund **passed** by **successive** U.S. **Presidential administrations**, but this is a bit **simplistic considering** these **policies** don't **mandate** the **sheer** number of tests students are asked to take these days. New York State, for example, has the one of the most exhaustive testing policies in the United States. The federal **legislation mentioned** above only **requires** students to be **evaluated** in English and Math in **grades** three through eight and once in high school. However, New York requires students take and pass five tests to **graduate**. Test **companies**, some believe, have **capitalized** on the need to teach for these tests by **providing** a broader **catalogue** of test prep **materials** and **courses**.

Vocabulary Building

Exercise A: Choose the option (**a**, **b**, **c** or **d**) which fits best each sentence.

1. The new director decided to ………. regular tests at school.

   a. blame   c. mention

   b. mandate   d. consider

2. I'll be shortly beginning a ………. on philosophy.

   a. grade   c. material

   b. catalogue   d. course

Exercise B: Fill in the blanks in the following sentences using the correct form of the words from the box below. There are 2 extra words in the box you do not need to use.

| a. pass | b. require | c. evaluate | d. graduate | e. capitalize | f. provide |

1. She ……graduated…… from college last year and she has already found a job.
2. I hope he …will capitalize/capitalizes… on the opportunity he is given by the company.
3. Students ……are required…… to attend classes regularly.
4. The House of Representatives insisted on ……passing…… the new Bill.

Exercise C: Fill in the definitions using words from the box below. There are 2 extra words in the box that you do not need to use.

| a. evolution | b. administration | c. policy | d. legislation | e. company | f. act |

1. ……Legislation…… is a proposed or enacted law.
2. ……Administration…… means the executive branch of the government.
3. ……Evolution…… refers to a development; often gradual.
4. ……Act…… is something which results from a legislative decision.

Exercise D: Fill in the chart with the derivatives of the given adjectives or adverbs. Then, provide one **synonym** and one **antonym**, taking into account their meaning in the specific text above.

	Verb	Noun	Adjective	Adverb
1.	succeed	successor / succession	successive	successively
2.	preside	president	presidential	presidentially
3.	simplify	simplification	simplistic	simplistically
4.	-	sheerness	sheer	sheerly

		Synonym	Antonym
1.	successive	consecutive/serial	discontinuous/inconsecutive
2.	presidential	statesmanlike	unpresidential
3.	simplistic	oversimplified/shallow	complicated
4.	sheer	total/complete	incomplete/partial

Exercise E: Write 4 sentences using the following words: complicated, unpresidential, discontinuous, incomplete. You must write 1 sentence for each of these words. Use between 8 and 15 words in each sentence.

(Suggested Answers)

1. The relationship between them has been very complicated over the past few years.
2. His behavior when meeting the foreign delegates was completely unpresidential.
3. The discontinuous nature of the country's economic development troubles analysts.
4. My paper is still incomplete; I need to write the conclusion.

Standardized Tests in School

Paragraph 4

A Some blame this evolution on the No Child Left Behind Act or Race to the Top Fund passed by successive U.S. Presidential administrations, but this is a bit **simplistic** considering these policies don't mandate the sheer number of tests students are asked to take these days. **B** New York State, for example, has the one of the most exhaustive testing policies in the United States. The federal legislation mentioned above only requires students to be evaluated in English and Math in grades three through eight and once in high school. **C** However, New York requires students take and pass five tests to graduate. Test companies, some believe, have capitalized on the need to teach for these tests by providing a broader catalogue of test prep materials and courses. **D**

Reading Comprehension

1. The word **simplistic** in §4 is closest in meaning to
   a. difficult.
   b. harsh.
   c. lacking depth.
   d. withholding.

2. Why does the author say that blaming Federal legislation for the current educational climate is misguided?
   a. States are mandating far more tests than the Federal government requires.
   b. Testing companies are shrinking their service and product offerings.
   c. New York State has implemented less testing for math and reading.
   d. The culture around testing has proved to be successful in increasing reading levels.

3. Why does the author refer to the No Child Left Behind or Race to the Top programs?
   a. to blame them as the single reason for the rise of the test culture in schools
   b. to show how these policies created richer curricula in schools
   c. to set up his larger argument on the forces behind the testing culture
   d. to debunk the perceived efficacy of these programs in improving education

4. Which sentence best expresses the essential information in the underlined sentence in §4?
   a. Test companies are losing money in the current educational environment.
   b. Test companies may be contributing to the emergence of this trend in education.
   c. Test companies should increase their offerings to better prepare teachers and students.
   d. Test companies are out of touch with the larger trends occurring in the educational landscape

5. All of the following are reasons the author believes testing has emerged so profoundly in schools **EXCEPT**
   a. state testing policies.
   b. test company financial motives.
   c. lack of teaching by parents.
   d. marketing of test prep classes.

6. Look at the four squares, **A**, **B**, **C** and **D**, which indicate where the following sentence could be added to the passage. Where would the sentence best fit?   Right Answer: D

These companies have introduced aggressive marketing campaigns in creating urgency for their products and services.

7. An introductory sentence for a brief summary of the passage is provided below. Complete the summary by selecting the **THREE** answer choices that express the most important ideas in the passage. Some sentences do not belong in the summary because they express ideas that are not presented in the passage or are ideas of minor importance. **This question is worth 2 points.**

Various factors are contributing to the rise of testing as the focus of educational practices in schools.

a. No Child Left Behind has made it harder for local governments to test.
b. State governments have introduced more testing as part of the educational requirements.
c. Private companies have created markets for test resources and preparation classes.
d. States like New York have made testing a pillar of education assessment.
e. Teachers have become outspoken advocates for more testing in schools.

Standardized Tests in School

Paragraph 5

Some experts have made **persuasive arguments** for how the emphasis on test scores has **commodified** education, thus **inducing motives** for people to try and cheat and/or **game** the system. For instance, **value**-added evaluations that result in pay **increases** for schools with higher test scores **incentivize** teachers and administrators to push the envelope and **refocus** their educational **approach** to the tests **exclusively**, thereby enhancing the **prospect** of **bettering** their **livelihoods** financially. In some cases, schools and teachers have been caught in cheating **scandals** driven by these financial motives in **doctoring** test scores and/or providing unfair **advantages** during the tests. More importantly, teachers and schools are becoming **rewarded**, even though their students are not receiving an **enriching** education. Given this **dynamic,** often those most prone to cheat to **benefit** from the system are the **weakest** teachers and school systems.

Vocabulary Building

Exercise A: Choose the option (a, b, c or d) which fits best each sentence.

1. There is little .... of having these questions answered.
   a. motive
   b. approach
   c. prospect
   d. dynamic

2. The economic crisis was .... by the high oil prices.
   a. induced
   b. rewarded
   c. incentivized
   d. benefited

Exercise B: Fill in the blanks in the following sentences using words from the box. You may need to change the word. There are 2 extra words in the box you do not need to use.

a. commodify	b. game	c. refocus	d. enrich	e. better	f. doctor

1. The criminal ......doctored...... the evidence to prove himself innocent in yesterday's trial.
2. You simply can't ......commodify...... art; it is not marketed.
3. ......Bettering...... conditions in prison is one of our main concerns.
4. We will have .....to refocus..... on our project if we want to meet the deadline.

Exercise C: Fill in the definitions using words from the box below. There are 2 extra words in the box that you do not need to use.

a. argument	b. value	c. increase	d. livelihood	e. scandal	f. advantage

1. ......Livelihood...... refers to the means of supporting one's existence.
2. ......Advantage...... is a benefit or profit.
3. ......Argument...... means a reason put forward as evidence.
4. ......Scandal...... is a situation which causes public outrage.

Exercise D: Fill in the chart with the derivatives of the given adjectives or adverbs. Then, provide one **synonym** and one **antonym**, taking into account their meaning in the specific text above.

	Verb	Noun	Adjective	Adverb
1.	persuade	persuasion	persuasive	persuasively
2.	enrich	enrichment	enriching	enrichingly
3.	weaken	weakness	weak	weakly
4.	exclude	exclusion	exclusive	exclusively

		Synonym	Antonym
1.	persuasive	convincing/effective	invalid/unconvincing
2.	enriching	enhancing/cultivating	impoverishing/depriving
3.	weak	inadequate/deficient	effective/efficient
4.	exclusively	solely/entirely	partially/moderately

Exercise E: Write 4 sentences using the following words: efficient, moderately, invalid, depriving. You must write 1 sentence for each of these words. Use between 8 and 15 words in each sentence. (Suggested Answers)

1. He is a highly efficient worker; that is why he is paid well.
2. The newly imported machines in the factory operated moderately well.
3. Your arguments are rendered invalid by the hard facts.
4. His state can only be described as simply depriving.

Standardized Tests in School

Paragraph 5

Some experts have made persuasive arguments for how the emphasis on test scores has commodified education, thus inducing motives for people to try and cheat and/or game the system. **A** For instance, value-added evaluations that result in pay increases for schools with higher test scores incentivize teachers and administrators to **push the envelope** and refocus their educational approach to the tests exclusively, thereby enhancing the prospect of bettering their livelihoods financially. **B** In some cases, schools and teachers have been caught in cheating scandals driven by these financial motives in doctoring test scores and/or providing unfair advantages during the tests. More importantly, teachers and schools are becoming rewarded, even though their students are not receiving an enriching education. **C** Given this dynamic, often those most prone to cheat to benefit from the system are the weakest teachers and school systems. **D**

Reading Comprehension

1. The phrase **push the envelope** in §5 is closest in meaning to
  a. take less risks.
  b. become more innovative.
  c. become less bold.
  d. avoid confrontation.

2. According to the text, how has the emphasis on test scores shaped the approach of educators?
  a. Teachers and schools are becoming more cautious in their approach.
  b. Teachers and schools have become more reckless in the quest for higher scores.
  c. The integrity of teachers and schools has become stronger in this educational environment.
  d. The integrity of the system has remained unblemished with the urgency for higher test performance.

3. Why does the writer mention the financial rewards for higher test scores for teachers and schools?
  a. to show why these professionals have been inclined to take less risks with their careers
  b. to illustrate that these professionals remain immune to any temptation to push the envelope
  c. to show how money has become a non-factor in evaluating student performance
  d. to illustrate why these professionals have been susceptible to questionable behavior

4. Which sentence below best expresses the essential information in the underlined sentence in §5?
  a. While educators benefit financially from the system, students are becoming better educated.
  b. The financial incentives in the system help students to perform better in all facets of their education.
  c. While educators gain in terms of money, students are receiving less viable education.
  d. The financial incentives in the current system are becoming more valuable as students and teachers perform better.

5. All of the following have resulted from the financial motives of testing **EXCEPT**
  a. cases of fraud.
  b. weak teachers cutting corners.
  c. alterations of test scores.
  d. more transparency in schools.

6. Look at the four squares, **A**, **B**, **C** and **D**, which indicate where the following sentence could be added to the passage. Where would the sentence best fit?　　　Right Answer: D

*In the end, without a complete overhaul to this approach, the risks
for future fraud and eroding educational standards grow.*

7. An introductory sentence for a brief summary of the passage is provided below. Complete the summary by selecting the **THREE** answer choices that express the most important ideas in the passage. Some sentences do not belong in the summary because they express ideas that are not presented in the passage or are ideas of minor importance. **This question is worth 2 points.**

*With such importance given to standardized testing, cheating scandals
have surfaced calling into question the testing culture.*

a. Teachers and administrators are tempted to bend the rules because higher test scores earn them more money.
b. Less capable teachers and poor performing schools don't feel the pressure to cheat on testing.
c. Educators have focused too much of their efforts on test preparation rather than broad learning.
d. Schools, under this model, are potentially receiving more money for test score performance, but students are not necessarily developing real skills.
e. The best teachers seek to change examination scores to receive salary bonuses.

Standardized Tests in School

Paragraph 6

Ultimately, under the **current circumstances**, schools may well become nothing more than test-preparation centers that **disregard** subject matters and skills that are not **measured** by the standardized **examinations**. Worse, this may well create a culture whereby teachers and administrators **resent** and/or **distrust** each other. Of course, teachers of high **integrity** and quality may well be lost or even **expunged** from the system. Furthermore, by making the test scores the **determining** factor for whether a school lives or dies, they have now become the **currency** by which all types of educational resources are being altered for the worse. Charter schools are eroding the role of traditional public schools. Online learning is becoming more **popular** than in-person **instruction** and **amateur** teachers are **replacing** more **experienced**, **tenured** instructors. Some of these changes may well be **beneficial**, but the **long-term** effects of making test the focus of education will **certainly erode** the skills and **capacity** of our citizens to lead our country in **coming** decades.

Vocabulary Building

Exercise A: Choose the option (**a**, **b**, **c** or **d**) which fits best each sentence.

1. Although it was a(n) .... cast the performance was brilliant.

   a. current

   b. replacing

   c. amateur

   d. coming

2. The cost is a(n) .... factor in our choice.

   a. experienced

   b. tenured

   c. long-term

   d. determining

Exercise B: Fill in the blanks in the following sentences using words from the box. You may need to change the word. There are 2 extra words in the box you do not need to use.

a. disregard	**b.** measure	**c.** resent	**d.** distrust	**e.** expunge	**f.** erode

1. This experience was something he tried to ......expunge...... from his memory.
2. ......Disregarding... the advice of his executives was not a smart move.
3. She definitely ......resents...... being dependent exclusively on him.
4. His recent indecisiveness ....has eroded.... his authority.

Exercise C: Fill in the definitions using words from the box below. There are 2 extra words in the box that you do not need to use.

a. circumstance	**b.** examination	**c.** integrity	**d.** currency	**e.** instruction	**f.** capacity

1. ......Integrity...... is adherence to moral principles; honesty.
2. ......Circumstance... means a condition or a series of facts.
3. ......Currency...... refers to general acceptance; prevalence.
4. ......Instruction.... is the act or practice of teaching.

Exercise D: Fill in the chart with the derivatives of the given adjectives or adverbs. Then, provide one **synonym** and one **antonym**, taking into account their meaning in the specific text above.

	Verb	Noun	Adjective	Adverb			Synonym	Antonym
1.	determine	determination	determining	determingly	**1.**	determining	important/essential	trivial/unimportant
2.	popularize	popularity	popular	popularly	**2.**	popular	well-liked	disliked
3.	ascertain	certainty	certain	certainly	**3.**	certainly	surely/definitely	questionably
4.	benefit	benefit	beneficial	beneficially	**4.**	beneficial	useful/valuable	harmful

Exercise E: Write 4 sentences using the following words: questionably, disliked, harmful, trivial. You must write 1 sentence for each of these words. Use between 8 and 15 words in each sentence. (Suggested Answers)

1. People say that he questionably acquired such wealth.
2. He was greatly disliked among his peers because of his behavior.
3. Ultra violet radiation is extremely harmful to one's skin.
4. Trivial matters do not require a lot of thought.

Debate 2

Standardized Tests in School

Paragraph 6

A Ultimately, under the current circumstances, schools may well become nothing more than test-preparation centers that disregard subject matters and skills that are not measured by the standardized examinations. <u>Worse, this may well create a culture whereby teachers and administrators resent and/or distrust each other.</u> **B** Of course, teachers of high integrity and quality may well be lost or even expunged from the system. Furthermore, by making the test scores the determining factor for whether a school lives or dies, they have now become the currency by which all types of educational resources are being altered for the worse. **C** Charter schools are **eroding** the role of traditional public schools. Online learning is becoming more popular than in-person instruction and amateur teachers are replacing more experienced, tenured instructors. **D** Some of these changes may well be beneficial, but the long-term effects of making test the focus of education will certainly erode the skills and capacity of our citizens to lead our country in coming decades.

Reading Comprehension

1. The word **eroding** in §6 is closest in meaning to
   a. strengthening.
   b. emboldening.
   c. undermining.
   d. increasing.

2. Based on the text, why is the current test trend in education a cause for concern?
   a. Teachers will become more honest and trusting in their profession.
   b. Students will receive an enriching education based on a diverse curriculum.
   c. Education will become too narrow in focus hurting the development of students.
   d. Schools will receive more money to better develop their teachers and students.

3. What does the author believe may happen to great teachers based on the current system?
   a. They will become even more prominent in schools.
   b. They will attract the best students to their classes.
   c. They will decide to leave private schools for public ones.
   d. They will, ironically, be lost from the system.

4. Which sentence below best expresses the essential information in the underlined sentence in §6?
   a. The current testing culture will cause possible division among educators.
   b. The current testing culture will bring teachers closer together.
   c. The current testing culture will enhance collaboration between professionals.
   d. The current test culture will foster rich inquiry among educators.

5. All of the following are results of standardized test emphasis **EXCEPT**
   a. animosity between teachers.
   b. great teachers staying in the profession.
   c. devaluing of public schools.
   d. more digital learning.

6. Look at the four squares, **A**, **B**, **C** and **D**, which indicate where the following sentence could be added to the passage. Where would the sentence best fit? Right Answer: B

   This type of animosity among professionals will only serve to undermine the performance of students further.

7. An introductory sentence for a brief summary of the passage is provided below. Complete the summary by selecting the **THREE** answer choices that express the most important ideas in the passage. Some sentences do not belong in the summary because they express ideas that are not presented in the passage or are ideas of minor importance. **This question is worth 2 points.**

   The Over-Emphasis on Testing has important consequences for education.

   a. Good teachers excel in the profession and advance.
   b. Online platforms replace live teaching.   B / C / F
   c. Curriculum becomes narrow and rigid.
   d. Teachers and parents work together to increase test scores.
   e. Students sign-up for more art and music courses.
   f. Teachers and administrators become more resentful of each other.

Standardized Tests: The Pros

Paragraph 1

Standardized tests make teachers **accountable** and benefit students. So, what's the problem? Certain political **factions** and teachers **unions** disagree with the usage of standardized testing in evaluating teacher, school and student performance, even though public support and **esteemed** experts in education have **underscored** the importance of such tests. Some of their most visible members have considered testing as "**infernal** machines of social destruction." Some politicians have also demonstrated a lack of **affinity** for the exams, as they believe the tests are far too simplistic or biased to truly evaluate the **nuances** education demands.

Paragraph 2

These arguments, though, are flimsy at best. History and research have clearly shown that standardized examinations are quite suitable for **fairly** and **objectively** evaluating the educational **enrichment** of a student. Outside of traditional schools, institutions of higher education and profession institutions have used them for decades to determine the **suitability** for a **candidate** in terms of **licensing** and advanced degrees. Indeed, if standardized tests are **applied poorly**, **inadequate** education for students may result. However, when applied correctly, they provide a wonderful measure for student, teacher and school achievement.

Paragraph 3

The information **gleaned** from tests enables authorities to determine areas requiring improvement in schools, while students receive **concrete feedback** on how well they've learned a given subject matter and in what areas they need further practice. Math and reading skills, for instance, can be measured and **subsequent** instruction can be developed **tailored** to meet these needs. Computer-based tests, of course, provide this feedback faster and more **efficiently** than humans can. In addition, skills beyond reading and math can be taught and evaluated, such as **composition** capabilities which can be broken down into sections on spelling, grammar, organization and style. Educational experts, in my opinion, should spend far less time **condemning** standardized tests and **invest** more time and energy into how they can use these tests to enhance the instruction they provide on a daily basis to their students.

Paragraph 4

Critics of the tests, moreover, believe that they result in neglecting other rich subject matters like history, science and foreign languages, all of which provide students with **invaluable** skills in their academic and professional lives. This, however, is an **argument** for broad testing for an entire **curriculum**, not one geared in **opposition** to standardized tests themselves. There are **plenty** of standardized tests, such as the AP Exams, that have been developed and **astutely** measure a student's skills in subjects like Chemistry and Spanish. With a little imagination and effort, I'm certain more **comprehensive** tests can be developed to evaluate the broader performance of students and teachers.

Paragraph 5

Detractors of standardized tests also **contend** that these exams can only measure **superficial** concepts that can easily be **committed** to memory. Yet, again, there are plenty of tests that evaluate sophisticated comprehension and analysis skills. Critics of these tests must spend less time finding **flaws** with the tests and more on solutions that better the educational performance of students within a standardized testing culture. I have no doubt that teachers and administrators can **collaborate** with educational institutions to develop tests that measure the necessary skills they believe are vital for students to develop in the digital age. As technology and the modern economy evolve, so should the skills schools **nurture** and evaluate in their students. This is not a time for **rigid**, fixed solutions, but rather an opportunity to establish a **fluid** approach to measuring performance and skill **acquisition.**

Paragraph 6

Progress in education in terms of the performance of schools, teachers and students must be measured empirically with standardized tests. These examinations benefit students and the system as a whole and should be **employed**, regardless if the matter does not achieve **unanimity** from the teaching community. When done right, standardized tests can provide a **lens** into the strengths and weaknesses of students, teachers and the system. They indicate when a student needs to be challenged more, when teachers need to **adjust** their approach and when schools require assistance or, better, **demand** recognition. These tests should not be the death **knell** for schools, but rather the **beacon** of light whereby achievement and lessons are recognized and shared across the educational community and society at large.

Debate 2

Vocabulary Building

Exercise A: Choose the option (**a**, **b**, **c** or **d**) which fits best each sentence.

1. His ………. for the job is unquestionable.
   a. suitability
   c. unanimity
   b. composition
   d. affinity

2. More people need to ……….. to fulfil the project.
   a. invest
   c. employ
   b. collaborate
   d. adjust

3. Your excuses prove once more to be ………. .
   a. esteemed
   c. inadequate
   b. infernal
   d. tailored

4. It is a(n) ………. easy problem to be solved.
   a. fairly
   c. efficiently
   b. poorly
   d. astutely

5. Maybe you should consider being less ………. in order to be liked.
   a. fluid
   c. superficial
   b. rigid
   d. plenty

6. I consider his loud voice to be a ………. that I can live with.
   a. beacon
   c. knell
   b. lens
   d. flaw

Exercise B: Fill in the blanks in the following sentences using words from the box. You may need to change the word. There are 2 extra words in the box you do not need to use.

a. underscore	b. apply	c. glean	d. condemn	e. contend	f. commit	g. nurture	h. demand

1. The criminal will be punished for the crime he ……committed…… .
2. The director's new film was greatly ……condemned…… for its inappropriate content.
3. ……Demanding…… in an impolite way to leave early is not acceptable.
4. There are certain exceptions where the rule does not always ……apply…… .
5. The doctor ……underscored…… a healthy diet and some exercise.
6. I would not advise you to ……glean…… random information from the newspapers.

Exercise C: Fill in the definitions using words from the box below. There are 2 extra words in the box that you do not need to use.

a. faction	b. nuance	c. enrichment	d. licensing	e. feedback	f. curriculum	g. opposition	h. detractor

1. ……Detractor…… is one who belittles the worth of something.
2. ……Feedback…… means an evaluative response on something done.
3. ……Faction…… refers to a minority of people in a larger group.
4. ……Enrichment…… is an act of making something fuller or more meaningful.
5. ……Nuance…… means a subtle difference or distinction.
6. ……Licensing…… is an act of providing official permission to do a specific thing.

Exercise D: Fill in the chart with the derivatives of the given adjectives or adverbs. Then, provide one **synonym** and one **antonym**, taking into account their meaning in the specific text above.

	Verb	Noun	Adjective	Adverb
1.	concretize	concretization	concrete	concretely
2.	sequence	(sub)sequence	subsequent	subsequently
3.	comprehend	comprehension	comprehensive	comprehensively
4.	-	objective	objective	objectively
5.	account	accountability	accountable	accountably
6.	value	value	invaluable	invaluably

		Synonym	Antonym
1.	concrete	specific	abstract
2.	subsequent	following	preceding
3.	comprehensive	broad/extensive	specialized/limited
4.	objectively	neutrally	subjectively
5.	accountable	responsible	irresponsible
6.	invaluable	valuable	worthless

Exercise E: Write 6 sentences using the following words: worthless, abstract, preceding, irresponsible, subjectively, specialized. You must write 1 sentence for each of these words. Use between 8 and 15 words in each sentence.

(Suggested Answers)

1. His guidelines were proven to be completely worthless.
2. Abstract notions are not always easy to comprehend.
3. You will find all necessary information in the preceding chapter.
4. It was very irresponsible of him to leave without informing us.
5. Subjectively, this artist's work is not going to be remembered for long.
6. Specialized tests can only show whether the candidate is suitable or not.

TOEFL Exam Practice: Reading Comprehension

Paragraph 1

Standardized tests make teachers **accountable** and benefit students. So, what's the problem? Certain political factions and teachers unions disagree with the usage of standardized testing in evaluating teacher, school and student performance, even though public support and esteemed experts in education have underscored the importance of such tests. Some of their most visible members have considered testing as "infernal machines of social destruction." Some politicians have also demonstrated a lack of affinity for the exams, as they believe the tests are far too simplistic or biased to truly evaluate the nuances education demands.

1. The word **accountable** in §1 is closest in meaning to
   a. unresponsive.
   b. neglected.
   c. responsible.
   d. distracted.

2. Based on the passage, why does the writer believe some are against standardized tests?
   a. They think the exams are too thorough in their approach.
   b. They believe the exams are not easy enough to prepare for and lack research to support their use.
   c. They believe the exams are not comprehensive enough in their approach.
   d. They think teachers change the test results to earn more money.

Paragraph 2

These arguments, though, are **flimsy** at best. History and research have clearly shown that standardized examinations are quite suitable for fairly and objectively evaluating the educational **enrichment** of a student. Outside of traditional schools, institutions of higher education and profession institutions have used them for decades to determine the suitability for a candidate in terms of licensing and advanced degrees. Indeed, if standardized tests are applied poorly, inadequate education for students may result. However, when applied correctly, they provide a wonderful measure for student, teacher and school achievement.

3. The word **flimsy** in §2 is closest in meaning to
   a. very strong.   c. lacking strength.
   b. difficult to understand.   d. easy to determine.

4. The word **enrichment** in §2 is closest in meaning to
   a. demotion.   c. decline.
   b. development.   d. determination.

5. Why does the author mention the use of standardized tests in universities and professional institutions?
   a. to show that they have no track record of efficacy
   b. to demonstrate that they are only effective in college admission settings
   c. to support his argument for their use in evaluating students and teachers
   d. to illustrate how the results of these tests are biased

Paragraph 3

The information **gleaned** from tests enables authorities to determine areas requiring improvement in schools, while students receive concrete feedback on how well they've learned a given subject matter and in what areas they need further practice. Math and reading skills, for instance, can be measured and subsequent instruction can be developed tailored to meet these needs. Computer-based tests, of course, provide this feedback faster and more efficiently than humans can. In addition, skills beyond reading and math can be taught and evaluated, such as composition capabilities which can be broken down into sections on spelling, grammar, organization and style. Educational experts, in my opinion, should spend far less time condemning standardized tests and invest more time and energy into how they can use these tests to enhance the instruction they provide on a daily basis to their students.

6. The word **gleaned** in §3 is closest in meaning to
   a. lost.
   b. permeated.
   c. harvested.
   d. misunderstood.

7. What does the author believe teachers should do with the standardized tests required for students?
   a. find methods to avoid them
   b. find ways to use them to better the advancement of their students
   c. find alternatives to them in testing student performance
   d. find optional venues for their usage outside of a traditional curriculum

Paragraph 4

Critics of the tests, moreover, believe that they result in neglecting other rich subject matters like history, science and foreign languages, all of which provide students with invaluable skills in their academic, professional and human lives. This, however, is an argument for broad testing for an entire curriculum, not one **geared** in opposition to standardized tests themselves. There are plenty of standardized tests, such as the AP Exams, that have been developed and astutely measure a student's skills in subjects like Chemistry and Spanish. With a little imagination and effort, I'm certain more comprehensive tests can be developed to evaluate the broader performance of students and teachers.

8. The word **geared** in §4 is closest in meaning to
   a. mislead.
   b. deconstructed.
   c. aimed.
   d. ridiculed.

9. Standardized tests can be used to evaluate
   a. only math and reading skills.
   b. a variety of rich subject matters beyond math and reading.
   c. math and reading skills but are more suited for foreign languages.
   d. a bevy of humanities based classes but not the sciences.

Paragraph 5

Detractors of standardized tests also contend that these exams can only measure superficial concepts that can easily be committed to memory. Yet, again, there are plenty of tests that evaluate sophisticated comprehension and analysis skills. Critics of these tests must spend less time finding flaws with the tests and more on solutions that better the educational performance of students within a standardized testing culture. I **have no doubt** that teachers and administrators can collaborate with educational institutions to develop tests that measure the necessary skills they believe are vital for students to develop in the digital age. As technology and the modern economy evolve, so should the skills schools nurture and evaluate in their students. This is not a time for rigid, fixed solutions, but rather an opportunity to establish a fluid approach to measuring performance and skill acquisition.

10. The phrase in §5 **have no doubt** is closest in meaning to
    a. don't know.
    b. strongly believe.
    c. question somebody's thoughts.
    d. wonder.

11. It can be inferred that the author
    a. thinks that teachers are correct in their criticism of standardized tests.
    b. underestimates how narrow the testing focus is.
    c. lacks a clear understanding of the arguments made in opposition to standardized testing.
    d. believes that teachers are underestimating their abilities in the testing culture.

12. All of the following are recommendations for teachers to adapt to the testing culture **EXCEPT**
    a. find more flaws with the approach.
    b. become seamless in their teaching style.
    c. open their mind to the system.
    d. work with other teachers and administrators to find solutions.

Paragraph 6

A Progress in education in terms of the performance of schools, teachers and students must be measured empirically with standardized tests. These examinations benefit students and the system as a whole and should be employed, regardless if the matter does not achieve **unanimity** from the teaching community. **B** When done right, standardized tests can provide a lens into the strengths and weaknesses of students, teachers and the system. They indicate when a student needs to be challenged more, when teachers need to adjust their approach and when schools require assistance or, better, demand recognition. **C** These tests should not be the death knell for schools, but rather the beacon of light whereby achievement and lessons are recognized and shared across the educational community and with society at large. **D**

13. The word **unanimity** in §6 is closest in meaning to
    a. discord.
    b. strong consensus.
    c. fractured thought.
    d. exposure.

14. Look at the four squares, **A**, **B**, **C** and **D**, which indicate where the following sentence could be added to the passage. Where would the sentence best fit? Right Answer: D

   Now more than ever a new standard must be established to ensure that our children are prepared to compete in an increasingly competitive global, economic environment.

Paragraphs 1 to 6

15. An introductory sentence for a brief summary of the passage is provided below. Complete the summary by selecting the **THREE** answer choices that express the most important ideas in the passage. Some sentences do not belong in the summary because they express ideas that are not presented in the passage or are ideas of minor importance. **This question is worth 2 points.**

   Standardized tests are an invaluable tool in measuring student and school performance in a time filled with rapid economic and technological change.

   a. These tests are needed to ensure that students and teachers are achieving at the necessary levels to succeed in contemporary times.
   b. Standardized tests fail to test a full range of skills needed in the global economy.
   c. The testing culture detracts from the overall enrichment of a student.
   d. Tests of this nature show where students need more help and when schools need to be acknowledged for excellence.
   e. Without standardized testing, it will become difficult to objectively measure the performance of the educational system.

Online Education

Paragraph 1

Though we are years into the **emergence** of online **forms** of education, many **perceptive** experts and students are still **skeptical** about the **quality** and **valuable** impact of this model, **based** on what has been **researched** from a **variety** of polling companies. Recently, the Hopkins Institute **polled** two groups with 5,000 people in each set to **determine** whether they believed digital forms of education were superior to more traditional forms. Those **surveyed** were asked whether they thought online was better than in-person, whether online **provided** a **bevy** of options for **curriculum** and whether it provided good value in terms of time and money. Based on these **criteria**, the online educational model **scored** slightly higher than traditional forms of education. At the same time, online educational methods **received** poorer **response**s in four other categories in terms of **delivering** tailored curriculum, quality of instruction from teachers, as well as in terms of providing fair and **comprehensive** **evaluation** and, most importantly, in terms of how the **degree** is **perceived** and valued by employers.

Vocabulary Building

Exercise A: Choose the option (**a**, **b**, **c** or **d**) which fits best each sentence.

1. The results of the experiment will .... its progress.
   a. determine   **c.** poll
   b. deliver   **d.** score

2. The .... of her classwork is very high.
   a. criterion   **c.** variety
   b. response   **d. quality**

Exercise B: Fill in the blanks in the following sentences using words from the box below. There are 2 extra words in the box you do not need to use. You cannot change the words.

a. base	b. survey	c. research	d. provide	e. receive	f. perceive

1. The scientists will ....receive..... funding in order to continue their project.
2. The university has offered to ......provide...... accommodation to students from abroad.
3. The postgraduate students should ......research..... the impact of using technology on learning.
4. His teachers ......perceive..... his poor performance as a sign of learning difficulties.

Exercise C: Fill in the definitions using words from the box below. There are 2 extra words in the box that you do not need to use.

a. emergence	b. curriculum	c. degree	d. form	e. evaluation	f. bevy

1. ....Curriculum.... is the detailed program of studies.
2. ....Evaluation.... is a process of assessment.
3. ....Bevy.... refers to a group of things.
4. ....Emergence.... means coming to surface or becoming visible.

Exercise D: Fill in the chart with the derivatives of the given adjectives or adverbs. Then, provide one **synonym** and one **antonym**, taking into account their meaning in the specific text above.

	Verb	Noun	Adjective	Adverb
1.	comprehend	comprehension/comprehensiveness	comprehensive	comprehensively
2.	–	skepticism	skeptical	skeptically
3.	perceive	perception	perceptive	perceptively
4.	value	value	valuable	valuably

		Synonym	Antonym
1.	comprehensive	extensive	limited
2.	skeptical	doubtful	convinced
3.	perceptive	observant	unobservant
4.	valuable	precious	valueless

Exercise E: Write 4 sentences using the following words: convinced, unobservant, valueless, limited. You must write 1 sentence for each of these words. Use between 8 and 15 words in each sentence. (Suggested Answers)

1. Some educators are convinced that e-learning is ideal for adult students.
2. He is described by his teachers as unobservant and passive.
3. Certificates are valueless if you do not have the necessary skills for the job.
4. They had limited access to the Internet when they were on the mountain.

Debate 3

Online Education

Paragraph 1

A Though we are years into the emergence of online forms of education, many perceptive experts and students are still **skeptical** about the quality and valuable impact of this model, based on what has been researched from a variety of polling companies. **B** Recently, the Hopkins Institute polled two groups with 5,000 people in each set to determine whether they believed digital forms of education were superior to more traditional forms. Those surveyed were asked and whether they thought online was better than in-person, whether online provided a bevy of options for curriculum and whether it provided good value in terms of time and money. **C** Based on these criteria, the online educational model scored slightly higher than traditional forms of education. **D** At the same time, online educational methods received poorer responses in four other categories in terms of delivering tailored curriculum, quality of instruction from teachers, as well as in terms of providing fair and comprehensive evaluation and, most importantly, in terms of how the degree is perceived and valued by employers.

Reading Comprehension

1. The word **skeptical** in §1 is closest in meaning to
   a. certain.
   b. remote.
   c. unconvinced.
   d. positive.

2. According to the passage, those surveyed found online learning to be superior to traditional education because
   a. the classes were given through video conference.
   b. the courses provided a good value in terms of content and cost.
   c. the classes only dealt with math, science and business courses.
   d. the courses didn't last too long during the semester.

3. Why have people found faults with online education?
   a. Because it only is available through the Internet.
   b. Because it traditionally serves those with a lot of money.
   c. Because most students prefer to learn in-person.
   d. Because employers don't seem to hold it in the same regard.

4. Which sentence below best expresses the essential information in the underlined sentence in §1?
   a. Within certain parameters, online education has proven to be somewhat better than traditional forms.
   b. Within certain parameters, traditional education has proven to be somewhat superior to online forms.
   c. Within certain parameters, online education has proven to favor the rich.
   d. Within certain parameters, traditional education has proven to lag far behind online learning.

5. All of the following have been considered weaknesses of online education **EXCEPT**
   a. tailored learning approach.
   b. standards of teaching.
   c. job placement.
   d. technological innovation.

6. Look at the four squares, **A**, **B**, **C** and **D**, which indicate where the following sentence could be added to the passage. Where would the sentence best fit?   Right Answer: A

   The digital age continues to evolve introducing new forms of technology that have transformed the way we live.

7. An introductory sentence for a brief summary of the passage is provided below. Complete the summary by selecting the **THREE** answer choices that express the most important ideas in the passage. Some sentences do not belong in the summary because they express ideas that are not presented in the passage or are ideas of minor importance. **This question is worth 2 points.**

   Online education is growing, but traditional education still maintains its dominance in the learning landscape.

   a. With traditional education, students don't develop long-term, personal relationships with their teachers.
   b. Online education platforms provide a medley of options for those looking to enhance their skills.
   c. Online education enables some students to get a useful education that is more cost effective.
   d. Teachers prefer to teach online than in-person so that they can reach more students.
   e. Companies still perceive traditional education as more attractive in potential employees.

Online Education

Paragraph 2

Thirty percent of the **participants** believed the online courses to be of **high** quality but 70 percent gave the same rating to **traditional** four-year universities, while 60 percent gave high **ratings** to community colleges and **related** institutions. These results **illustrate** that traditional forms of education are considered superior to online education in some of the most important ways. Andrea Smith, a director at the Hopkins Institute, found these results **particularly intriguing**. Smith especially **noted** the **significant** number of people who thought traditional forms of education were better **suited** to the **development** of the **individual** student, even though the most **ardent proponents** of online education **trumpet** the **personalized approach** as one of its **chief** benefits. The **evidence** ultimately suggests that people do not **perceive** this **supposed** advantage.

Vocabulary Building

Exercise A: Choose the option (**a**, **b**, **c** or **d**) which fits best each sentence.

1. She has always been a(n) ………. supporter of animal rights.
   a. personalized
   b. intriguing
   c. ardent
   d. chief

2. The teacher attributed the ………. rates of success to the student's effort.
   a. traditional
   b. high
   c. individual
   d. related

Exercise B: Fill in the blanks in the following sentences using words from the box below. There are 2 extra words in the box you do not need to use. You cannot change the words.

a. illustrate	b. note	c. suit	d. trumpet	e. perceive	f. intrigue

1. The results of the survey clearly ……illustrate…… the impact of the crisis on the population.
2. This afternoon course has been designed to ……suit…… the needs of students who work in the mornings.
3. The ministry will ……trumpet…… the new measures as a major reform.
4. The reader should ……note…… that general conclusions cannot be drawn.

Exercise C: Fill in the definitions using words from the box below. There are 2 extra words in the box that you do not need to use.

a. development	b. proponent	c. ratings	d. participant	e. approach	f. evidence

1. ……Proponent…… is a supporter of a theory or movement.
2. ……Approach…… means the way one deals with an issue.
3. ……Ratings…… refers to the percentage resulting from a survey.
4. ……Evidence…… is the data that proves a theory.

Exercise D: Fill in the chart with the derivatives of the given adjectives or adverbs. Then, provide one **synonym** and one **antonym**, taking into account their meaning in the specific text above.

	Verb	Noun	Adjective	Adverb			Synonym	Antonym
1.	suppose	supposition	supposed	supposedly	1.	supposed	perceived	factual
2.	signify	signification	significant	significantly	2.	significant	important	insignificant
3.	intrigue	intrigue	intriguing	intriguingly	3.	intriguing	thought-provoking	unexciting
4.	part / particularize	part / particularity	particular	particularly	4.	particularly	specifically	generally

Exercise E: Write 4 sentences using the following words: insignificant, unexciting, factual, generally. You must write 1 sentence for each of these words. Use between 8 and 15 words in each sentence. (Suggested Answers)

1. The details he focused on were insignificant and did not make a difference.
2. People often believe that scientists lead an unexciting life.
3. This course focuses on factual writing and not on fiction.
4. His work is generally acceptable by the scientific community.

Debate 3

Online Education

Paragraph 2

A Thirty percent of the participants believed the online courses to be of high quality but 70 percent gave the same rating to traditional four-year universities, while 60 percent gave high ratings to community colleges and related institutions. **B** <u>These results illustrate that traditional forms of education are considered superior to online education in some of the most important ways.</u> **C** Andrea Smith, a director at the Hopkins Institute, found these results particularly intriguing. Smith especially noted the significant number of people who thought traditional forms of education were better suited to the development of the individual student, even though the most ardent proponents of online education **trumpet** the personalized approach as one of its chief benefits. The evidence ultimately suggests that people do not perceive this supposed advantage. **D**

Reading Comprehension

1. The word **trumpet** in §2 is closest in meaning to
   a. disregard.
   c. persuade.
   b. promote.
   d. instrument.

2. Based on the text, how have survey participants evaluated the benefits of traditional education?
   a. They ironically see it as superior in developing a personalized educational approach.
   b. They foolishly believe it is inferior to online learning platforms.
   c. They mistakenly think online education will become obsolete in the future.
   d. They interestingly undermine the ability of teachers to teach a variety of subjects.

3. Why does the writer mention the findings of the expert at the research organization?
   a. to discredit professors who teach in traditional universities
   b. to undermine the reputation of a traditional college education
   c. to support arguments on the value of traditional learning
   d. to advocate for online learning to replace traditional schools

4. Which sentence below expresses the essential information in the underlined sentence in §2?
   a. Online education has gone beyond the advances in traditional learning environments.
   b. Online education has become the learning mode of choice for students.
   c. Traditional learning, based on the evidence, still holds value over online education.
   d. Traditional learning has become unpopular among digital entrepreneurs.

5. All of the following are true regarding the survey results **EXCEPT**
   a. sixty percent of the participants believe online learning is overrated.
   b. seventy percent of participants find value in college education.
   c. sixty percent of those surveyed find value in community learning institutions.
   d. thirty percent of those surveyed find value in online learning platforms.

6. Look at the four squares, **A**, **B**, **C** and **D**, which indicate where the following sentence could be added to the passage. Where would the sentence best fit?   Right Answer: D

   Therefore, it seems that little risk exists for traditional schools to be replaced by online learning platforms.

7. An introductory sentence for a brief summary of the passage is provided below. Complete the summary by selecting the **THREE** answer choices that express the most important ideas in the passage. Some sentences do not belong in the summary because they express ideas that are not presented in the passage or are ideas of minor importance. **This question is worth 2 points.**

   Studies have found that, despite the perception, traditional learning is still valued over online platforms.

   a. More people are choosing to study through online portals than attending traditional colleges.
   b. Fewer students see the benefits of traditional colleges given the cost of tuition.
   c. Traditional educational institutions still hold significant value in the educational landscape.
   d. A vast majority of students polled see universities and colleges as worthwhile institutions for learning.
   e. Ironically, students see traditional learning classrooms as more personal than online educational platforms.

Online Education

Paragraph 3

The research study **established** that only 4 percent of the **citizenry** as well as 18 percent of university students had **registered** for an online class. This **trend reflects**, in Smith's **viewpoint**, that people have **adopted** online educational **offerings** but that it has not **gained sufficient** support to **replace** traditional forms of education in the near future. Nevertheless, advocates and executives of **leading** online educational institutions **maintain** that their **vehicles** are superior, given the price and **rigid** approach of traditional colleges, universities and other forms of education. At a **recent** educational **conference**, one director from an online school went as far as to **speculate** that **digital** forms of education are the only solution for people looking to be **prepared** to **compete** in the digital age.

Vocabulary Building

Exercise A: Choose the option (**a**, **b**, **c** or **d**) which fits best each sentence.

1. The university has complained that it does not receive .... funding.
   a. recent   c. rigid
   b. digital   **d. sufficient**

2. The change of policy .... the latest developments in the field.
   a. reflects   c. adopts
   b. replaces   d. prepares

Exercise B: Fill in the blanks in the following sentences using the correct form of the words from the box below. There are 2 extra words in the box you do not need to use.

| a. gain | b. register | c. speculate | d. compete | e. maintain | f. establish |

1. A large number of students .....registered.... for a webinar on this course.
2. Recently the reforms in education ...have gained.... the support of school teachers.
3. The organization ...speculates..... that the rate of illiteracy will double this year.
4. He ....maintained.... that his project was innovative but few people agreed.

Exercise C: Fill in the definitions using words from the box below. There are 2 extra words in the box that you do not need to use.

| a. trend | b. viewpoint | c. citizenry | d. conference | e. offering | f. vehicle |

1. .....Vehicle..... refers to the medium used to convey ideas and beliefs.
2. .....Trend..... is the tendency to adopt an approach.
3. .....Viewpoint..... means the opinion one has on an issue.
4. .....Conference..... is a type of convention where many people meet to exchange ideas.

Exercise D: Fill in the chart with the derivatives of the given adjectives or adverbs. Then, provide one **synonym** and one **antonym**, taking into account their meaning in the specific text above.

	Verb	Noun	Adjective	Adverb
1.	-	rigidness	rigid	rigidly
2.	lead	leader/leadership	leading	leadingly
3.	digit(al)ize	digit(alization)	digital	digitally
4.	suffice	sufficiency / sufficer	sufficient	sufficiently

		Synonym	Antonym
1.	rigid	firm	flexible
2.	leading	top/outstanding	minor/secondary
3.	digital	computerized	handwritten
4.	sufficient	ample	insufficient

Exercise E: Write 4 sentences using the following words: flexible, handwritten, insufficient, secondary. You must write 1 sentence for each of these words. Use between 8 and 15 words in each sentence.

(Suggested Answers)

1. Our university offers flexible programs of studies for people who work.
2. Handwritten assignments will not be accepted.
3. His thesis had insufficient evidence and therefore he failed.
4. The equipment in our computer lab is outdated.

Online Education

Paragraph 3

A The research study established that only 4 percent of the citizenry as well as 18 percent of university students had registered for an online class. This trend **reflects**, in Smith's viewpoint, that people have adopted online educational offerings but that it has not gained sufficient support to replace traditional forms of education in the near future. **B** Nevertheless, advocates and executives of leading online educational institutions maintain that their vehicles are superior, given the price and rigid approach of traditional colleges, universities and other forms of education. **C** At a recent educational conference, one director from an online school went as far as to speculate that digital forms of education are the only solution for people looking to be prepared to compete in the digital age. **D**

Reading Comprehension

1. The word **reflects** in §3 is closest in meaning to
   a. retreads.
   c. illustrates.
   b. involves.
   d. undermines.

2. According to the passage, why did the director of an online educational institution argue that such institutions are superior?
   a. Because they are less suited for the digital age.
   b. Because they offer the best preparation for the technological era.
   c. Because they provide rich humanities based instruction.
   d. Because few students have the patience and time to attend traditional lectures.

3. Why does the writer discuss the percentages of people who have signed up for an online course?
   a. to show that many students prefer online learning over traditional classrooms
   b. to illustrate that many people are dropping out of traditional universities
   c. to show that not a significant number of people are enrolling in online courses
   d. to illustrate that few students prefer traditional settings over online platforms

4. Which sentence best expresses the essential information in the underlined sentence in §3?
   a. Those that run online education platforms see them as better for students because of their flexibility and cost.
   b. Those that run online education platforms see them as an industry in decline.
   c. Those that run online education platforms see them as overvalued compared to traditional schools.
   d. Those that run online education platforms see them as appropriate only for remedial students.

5. All of the following are reasons directors advocate online education **EXCEPT**
   a. affordable cost.
   b. tailored instruction.
   c. offline applications.
   d. flexible approach.

6. Look at the four squares, **A**, **B**, **C** and **D**, which indicate where the following sentence could be added to the passage. Where would the sentence best fit?

Right Answer: A

The data on the trend illustrates an online adoption rate lower than some would expect.

7. An introductory sentence for a brief summary of the passage is provided below. Complete the summary by selecting the **THREE** answer choices that express the most important ideas in the passage. Some sentences do not belong in the summary because they express ideas that are not presented in the passage or are ideas of minor importance. **This question is worth 2 points.**

Despite popular perception, online education still has to make great strides to catch up with the dominance of traditional learning platforms.

   a. More students are choosing to learn online versus going to traditional colleges.
   b. A small percentage of students have registered for online courses.
   c. Professors prefer to teach online than in-person to a room of students.
   d. Online learning executives trumpet the flexibility and cost efficiency of their institutions.
   e. Digital educational platform advocates believe online learning is crucial for students to excel in the age of the Internet and other wired technologies.

Online Education

Paragraph 4

To **further** this idea, one **executive eagerly remarked** that within 30 to 40 years, all but 500 or so **traditional** universities will **undoubtedly** be closed. This trend, though, **seemed remote considering** the **input** of **current** students who **valued** live, in-person **instruction**. They wanted their teachers to be **fluent** and **comfortable** with technology; yet, they considered online forms of education difficult to **negotiate** and **overvalued**. Students found that online forms of learning made it easy for students to **cheat** and **questioned** the **quality** and **value** of the education **provided**. Moreover, in their opinion, traditional forms of education offered the **opportunity** to network and connect with fellow students and teachers. This is something online education could not provide in the eyes of many students.

Vocabulary Building

Exercise A: Choose the option (**a**, **b**, **c** or **d**) which fits best each sentence.

1. The instructor decided to ………. his idea and offer courses for everyone.
   - **a.** seem
   - **b. further**
   - **c.** consider
   - **d.** provide

2. He is ………. in three languages.
   - **a.** current
   - **b.** remote
   - **c.** traditional
   - **d. fluent**

Exercise B: Fill in the blanks in the following sentences using the correct form of the words from the box below. There are 2 extra words in the box you do not need to use.

a. cheat	**b.** remark	**c.** value	**d.** negotiate	**e.** overvalue	**f.** question

1. The university scientists ..are questioning.. the validity of the researcher's methods now.
2. The potential of technology can be …overvalued….. compared to what it can actually achieve.
3. The teacher did not negotiate the amount of work she assigned. She would not even think about it.
4. He ……remarked….. that it was too early to reach conclusions about the program's effectiveness.

Exercise C: Fill in the definitions using words from the box below. There are 2 extra words in the box that you do not need to use.

a. executive	**b.** input	**c.** instruction	**d.** quality	**e.** value	**f.** opportunity

1. …..Opportunity…. is a chance offered to someone.
2. ……Quality……. refers to the aspect that determines the standard of work.
3. ……Executive…… means a high ranking person in a company.
4. ……Input……… is the unprocessed data humans or computers process.

Exercise D: Fill in the chart with the derivatives of the given adjectives or adverbs. Then, provide one **synonym** and one **antonym**, taking into account their meaning in the specific text above.

	Verb	Noun	Adjective	Adverb
1.	-	eagerness	eager	eagerly
2.	doubt	doubt	undoubted	undoubtedly
3.	-	fluency	fluent	fluently
4.	comfort	comfort	comfortable	comfortably

		Synonym	Antonym
1.	eagerly	passionately/ardently	indifferently
2.	undoubtedly	certainly/definitely	questionably/doubtfully
3.	fluent	competent	inarticulate
4.	comfortable	convenient	uncomfortable

Exercise E: Write 4 sentences using the following words: uncomfortable, doubtfully, indifferently, inarticulate. You must write 1 sentence for each of these words. Use between 8 and 15 words in each sentence.

(Suggested Answers)

1. She felt very uncomfortable when her classmate insulted her.
2. He examined our proposal very doubtfully as he was not at all convinced.
3. She looked at me very indifferently as if she did not know me.
4. His inarticulate speech made communication between us impossible.

Online Education

Paragraph 4

A To further this idea, one executive eagerly remarked that within 30 to 40 years, all but 500 or so traditional universities will undoubtedly be closed. This idea, though, seemed **remote** considering the input of current students who valued live, in-person instruction. **B** They wanted their teachers to be fluent and comfortable with technology; yet, they considered online forms of education difficult to negotiate and overvalued. Students found that online forms of learning made it easy for students to cheat and questioned the quality and value of the education provided. **C** Moreover, in their opinion, traditional forms of education offered the opportunity to network and connect with fellow students and teachers. This is something online education could not provide in the eyes of many students. **D**

Reading Comprehension

1. The word **remote** in §4 is closest in meaning to
   a. close.
   b. plausible.
   c. arbitrary.
   d. unlikely.

2. Based on the passage, why do students value traditional forms of education over online portals?
   a. It's easier to cheat on tests in traditional classrooms.
   b. The professors provide more personal attention to students in digital learning arenas.
   c. Traditional classrooms enable students to receive personal guidance from their teachers.
   d. Online platforms lack the flexibility for students to tailor their learning.

3. Why does the writer refer to the comments made by the online educational executive?
   a. to dismiss the relevancy of traditional classroom instruction
   b. to show that teachers need to be more personal with their students
   c. to illustrate the growing reliance on computers in society
   d. to set up the arguments to counter the claim by the individual

4. Which sentence best expresses the essential information in the underlined sentence in §4?
   a. Students liked it when teachers were capable of using technology, but didn't think online education was more effective.
   b. Students disagreed when teachers relied on tailored and in-person instruction.
   c. Students enjoyed it when teachers stressed digital forms of learning on the Internet.
   d. Students saw limits to the effectiveness of in-person education especially when teachers weren't fluent in computer applications.

5. All of the following are reasons the writer thinks students favor traditional education **EXCEPT**
   a. relationships with other students.
   b. mentorship from teachers.
   c. it is harder to cheat with online education.
   d. it is easier to execute.

6. Look at the four squares, **A**, **B**, **C** and **D**, which indicate where the following sentence could be added to the passage. Where would the sentence best fit?

Right Answer: D

So, the viewpoints of online educational insiders aside, it seems that the position of traditional educational platforms is safe.

7. An introductory sentence for a brief summary of the passage is provided below. Complete the summary by selecting the **THREE** answer choices that express the most important ideas in the passage. Some sentences do not belong in the summary because they express ideas that are not presented in the passage or are ideas of minor importance. **This question is worth 2 points.**

Students prefer the traditional classroom setting over online educational platforms.

a. Online education doesn't provide the same quality of instruction or integrity.
b. In-person instruction enables students to make contacts and receive mentoring from teachers.
c. Online classes are easier for students to navigate logistically.
d. In-person classrooms have become obsolete in the digital era.
e. Academic honesty is valued higher in traditional classroom settings.

Online Education

Paragraph 5

Along these **lines**, **traditional** educational **forms** offer **benefits** that digital forms cannot **simulate**. Given the human beings are social beings, receiving an education in **seclusion** is difficult. In a traditional learning environment, students learn to **socialize** with their teachers and contemporaries, which is something difficult to simulate online without in-person **contact**. **Experts** believe that developing these people skills are **imperative**, as humans **progress** with the help of others. Professors also teach other skills in-person, such as study skills and timeliness, as well as providing **guidance** for life choices outside of the classroom. In other words, the human contact with teachers offers **mentorship** opportunities and **insight** into life that are difficult to **establish** online. Students may well **miss** out on valuable guidance and/or **lucrative** and **enriching** career **opportunities** that may **transform** their life.

Vocabulary Building

Exercise A: Choose the option (**a**, **b**, **c** or **d**) which fits best each sentence.

1. We will deal with other students along similar ....
  a. opportunities   **c. lines**
  b. experts   **d.** forms

2. Online courses are a very .... business with profits riching millions of dollars.
  a. lucrative   **c.** enriching
  b. imperative   **d.** traditional

Exercise B: Fill in the blanks in the following sentences using words from the box. You may need to change the word. There are 2 extra words in the box you do not need to use.

a. simulate	**b.** socialize	**c.** progress	**d.** establish	**e.** miss	**f.** transform

1. Mock exams are aiming at ......simulating.... an examination environment.
2. The introduction of technology in schools some years ago ....transformed... the way we perceive education.
3. John is excellent when it comes to ....socializing.. . He is a very outgoing person.
4. The project ....progresses.... slowly but we will meet the deadline.

Exercise C: Fill in the definitions using words from the box below. There are 2 extra words in the box that you do not need to use.

a. insight	**b.** mentorship	**c.** guidance	**d.** seclusion	**e.** benefit	**f.** contact

1. ......Benefit...... refers to an advantage one has.
2. ......Insight...... means important knowledge to understand how something works.
3. ......Seclusion.... is the state of being away from people.
4. ......Guidance...... is the help one receives to understand something.

Exercise D: Fill in the chart with the derivatives of the given adjectives or adverbs. Then, provide one **synonym** and one **antonym**, taking into account their meaning in the specific text above.

	Verb	Noun	Adjective	Adverb
1.	value	value	valuable	valuably
2.	enrich	enrichment	enriching	enrichingly
3.	-	imperative	imperative	imperatively
4.	humanize	human/humanity	human	humanly

		Synonym	Antonym
1.	valuable	precious	valueless
2.	enriching	supplementing	impoverishing
3.	imperative	essential/crucial	optional/unnecessary
4.	human	man-centered	inhuman

Exercise E: Write 4 sentences using the following words: valueless, impoverishing, optional, inhuman. You must write 1 sentence for each of these words. Use between 8 and 15 words in each sentence.

(Suggested Answers)

1. This antique clock, contrary to what one might believe, is valueless.
2. War always has an impoverishing effect on countries.
3. There are optional assignments you can chose as extra-credit.
4. We should not tolerate such an inhuman treatment of animals

Debate 3

Online Education

Paragraph 5

A Along these lines, traditional educational forms offer benefits that digital forms cannot simulate. <u>Given the human beings are social beings, receiving an education through seclusion is difficult.</u> **B** In a traditional learning environment, students learn to socialize with their teachers and **contemporaries**, which is something difficult to simulate online without in-person contact. **C** Experts believe that developing these people skills are imperative, as humans progress with the help of others. Professors also teach other skills in-person, such as study skills and timeliness, as well as providing guidance for life choices outside of the classroom. In other words, the human contact with teachers offers mentorship opportunities and insight into life that are difficult to establish online. Students may well miss out on valuable guidance and/or lucrative and enriching career opportunities that may transform their life. **D**

Reading Comprehension

1. The word **contemporaries** in §5 is closest in meaning to
   a. enemies.
   b. assistants.
   c. peers.
   d. acquaintances.

2. Based on the passage, what does traditional instruction offer than cannot be attained with online classes?
   a. It provides relationship-building opportunities with teachers and students.
   b. It helps students rely more on books than computers.
   c. It maximizes a student's ability to master new forms of technology.
   d. It facilitates the teacher's ability to reach students at any time in any part of the world.

3. Why does the author discuss the development of social skills in his argument?
   a. to show traits that online education helps a student attain
   b. to illustrate ways in which traditional classrooms are superior to online platforms
   c. to discredit traditional classrooms from this view-point compared to what online platforms offer
   d. to explain why these skills are overvalued in the digital era

4. Which sentence below best expresses the essential information in the underlined sentence in §5?
   a. Because the nature of humans is to be isolated from each other, online education suits this dynamic.
   b. Because humans shun interaction, traditional forms of education are not suitable any longer.
   c. Because people tend to think in herds, online education helps them to think for themselves.
   d. Because humans interact greatly, traditional educational settings are important in developing social skills.

5. All of the following are considered skills taught in traditional classrooms **EXCEPT**
   a. punctuality.
   b. social development.
   c. mentoring.
   d. social media abilities.

6. Look at the four squares, **A**, **B**, **C** and **D**, which indicate where the following sentence could be added to the passage. Where would the sentence best fit?   Right Answer: A

   Let's not foolishly limit our teachers into rigid roles of simply instructing academic subject matters.

7. An introductory sentence for a brief summary of the passage is provided below. Complete the summary by selecting the **THREE** answer choices that express the most important ideas in the passage. Some sentences do not belong in the summary because they express ideas that are not presented in the passage or are ideas of minor importance. **This question is worth 2 points.**

   In-person instruction helps to nurture meaningful learning relationships between students and teachers.

   a. Teachers find it difficult to connect with students during live in-person classroom instruction.
   b. Students receive mentoring and broad life lessons from in-person teachers.
   c. The role of educators should be limited strictly to teaching academic subjects.
   d. Students benefit from exposure to life experiences that great teachers possess.
   e. In-person teaching helps students to develop more abstract life skills.

Debate 3

Online Education

Paragraph 6

In this regard, in-person teachers provide a **solid value** system for students, namely younger ones, of how to **behave** and carry themselves. Teachers can **serve** as great **role** models for students leaving an **impression** that they will carry for the **duration** of their **life, instilling** in them right from wrong and how to **negotiate delicate** matters. Furthermore, teachers and students can develop **bonds** that are extremely difficult to develop over the Internet. The role of teachers should **transcend** merely instructing academic subject matters and **encompass** sharing life lessons and teaching about matters that go beyond the classroom such as **real** world experiences such as travel, artistic **pursuits** and other related **professional** or **creative endeavors**. Given these **attributes**, parents and students should prefer traditional forms of education over **sterile** online forms.

Vocabulary Building

Exercise A: Choose the option (**a, b, c** or **d**) which fits best each sentence.

1. Learning difficulties are a ………. matter to deal with.
    a. delicate
    b. sterile
    c. creative
    d. professional

2. He acted as a ………. model for all his students.
    a. life
    b. role
    c. value
    d. real

Exercise B: Fill in the blanks in the following sentences using words from the box. You may need to change the word. There are 2 extra words in the box you do not need to use.

a. behave	**b.** transcend	**c.** encompass	**d.** instill	**e.** negotiate	**f.** serve

1. He ……served…….. as a head teacher at the local school for five years before retiring.
2. Innovation in education …..transcends….. limits and broadens our horizons.
3. Fortunately, our school teacher …..instilled…… necessary values for our lives.
4. He ……behaves….. as if he has never seen a computer before.

Exercise C: Fill in the definitions using words from the box below. There are 2 extra words in the box that you do not need to use.

a. duration	**b.** bond	**c.** pursuit	**d.** attribute	**e.** endeavor	**f.** impression

1. …..Duration…….. is the length of time that something lasts.
2. …..Pursuit…….. is an effort to gain or the quest to achieve something.
3. …..Bond…….. refers to a close relationship one establishes with friends and relatives.
4. …..Attribute…… means a personal quality or characteristic.

Exercise D: Fill in the chart with the derivatives of the given adjectives or adverbs. Then, provide one **synonym** and one **antonym**, taking into account their meaning in the specific text above.

	Verb	Noun	Adjective	Adverb
1.	-	delicacy/ delicateness	delicate	delicately
2.	create	creation	creative	creatively
3.	sterilize	sterilization	sterile	-
4.	solidify	solidity/solidness	solid	solidly

		Synonym	Antonym
1.	delicate	frail	gross
2.	creative	imaginative	unimaginative
3.	sterile	infertile	fertile
4.	solid	sound/substantial	precarious/decaying

Exercise E: Write 4 sentences using the following words: unimaginative, precarious, fertile, gross. You must write 1 sentence for each of these words. Use between 8 and 15 words in each sentence. (Suggested Answers)

1. His latest work has been labeled as completely unimaginative.
2. His solution to the problem was a very precarious option.
3. Her ideas found fertile ground among other thinkers.
4. He could only give a gross number of students attending his lecture regularly.

Debate 3

Online Education

Paragraph 6

A In this regard, in-person teachers provide a value system for students, namely younger ones, of how to behave and carry themselves. Teachers can serve as great role models for students leaving an impression that they will carry for the duration of their life, instilling in them right from wrong and how to negotiate **delicate** matters. B Furthermore, teachers and students can develop bonds that are extremely difficult to develop over the Internet. The role of teachers should transcend merely instructing academic subject matters and encompass sharing life lessons and teaching about matters that go beyond the classroom such as real world experiences such as travel, artistic pursuits and other related professional or creative endeavors. C Given these attributes, parents and students should prefer traditional forms of education over sterile online forms. D

Reading Comprehension

1. The word **delicate** in §6 is closest in meaning to
   a. obscene.
   b. harsh.
   c. sensitive.
   d. sturdy.

2. According to the passage, why should students and their families value traditional learning settings versus online ones?
   a. Students receive broad life lessons that cannot be simulated online.
   b. Students benefit from the cutting-edge digital platforms in classroom learning.
   c. Students are able to rely less on their parents for help with their assignments.
   d. Students find it easier to prepare for examinations with a live teacher.

3. What does the writer think the job of teachers should be?
   a. to simply teach academic subject matters based on their expertise
   b. to exclusively teach life lessons that can be applied across disciplines
   c. to complement traditional subject learning with broad worldly lessons.
   d. to focus on technological skills that will serve students in the digital era.

4. Which sentence best expresses the essential information in the underlined sentence in §6?
   a. Online education facilitates a student's ability to network with teachers and students.
   b. Online education enables students to receive the latest trends in digital education.
   c. Online education fails to enable students and teachers to connect meaningfully.
   d. Online education lacks the platform for teachers to convey complex lessons.

5. All of the following are reasons for students and parents to prefer traditional classroom settings **EXCEPT**
   a. technological advancement.
   b. life lessons.
   c. exposure to culture.
   d. mentoring opportunities.

6. Look at the four squares, A, B, C and D, which indicate where the following sentence could be added to the passage. Where would the sentence best fit?   Right Answer: B

   In other words, teachers can serve as an extension of the value system students receive from their parents.

7. Select the appropriate sentences from the answer choices and match them to the relationship between traditional classroom settings and student development. **TWO** of the answer choices will **NOT** be used. **This question is worth 3 points.**

   a. Students receive mentorship from professors with broad experience.
   b. Teachers share with students cultural and life experiences beyond subject learning.
   c. Students and teachers fail to develop close relationships.
   d. Outdated digital platforms prove harder to replace for new teachers.
   e. It becomes more difficult for teachers to be role models for children.
   f. New technologies make it harder for teachers to connect online with students.
   g. Teachers reinforce morals and values parents teach their children.

Benefit of Traditional Classrooms:	A/B/G
Drawback of Online Education:	C/E

Online Education

Paragraph 7

Online education has **become** a visible **trend** in contemporary times. In fact, students may well one day learn **exclusively** from their home-based computers instead of **attending** traditional schools in person. Of course, there has been some **successful** learning **accomplished** through this form of learning, such as with English-language lessons, whereby students and teachers use online **chats**, Skype and **accompanying headsets** to **facilitate** communication and education. At the **same** time, the advantages of traditional forms of education far **exceed** those of online **methods**. Students **acquire social** and life **skills** that cannot be **achieved** through **simple** online lessons. They are able to **connect** and learn from in-person **classmates** and teachers that **enrich** their lives with **lasting** relationships and guidance.

Vocabulary Building

Exercise A: Choose the option (**a**, **b**, **c** or **d**) which fits best each sentence.

1. His reforms have had a(n) ……. impact on education.
   a. same
   b. accompanying
   c. lasting
   d. simple

2. He ………. life skills by traveling all over the world.
   a. acquired
   b. accomplished
   c. accompanied
   d. connected

Exercise B: Fill in the blanks in the following sentences using words from the box. You may need to change the word. There are 2 extra words in the box you do not need to use.

| **a.** achieve | **b.** become | **c.** accomplish | **d.** exceed | **e.** enrich | **f.** facilitate |

1. He worked hard and ……achieved…… his goals.
2. Technology is believed to ……facilitate…… learning by providing easy access to data.
3. Soon her performance ……will exceed…… her professor's expectations.
4. In order to ……accomplish…… the task, you will have to work consistently.

Exercise C: Fill in the definitions using words from the box below. There are 2 extra words in the box that you do not need to use.

| **a.** trend | **b.** chat | **c.** headset | **d.** method | **e.** skill | **f.** classmate |

1. ……Chat…… means an informal discussion usually on the social media.
2. ……Classmate…… is a fellow student/pupil at school.
3. ……Method…… refers to a procedure followed to achieve a goal.
4. ……Skill…… is the ability in the form of knowledge one has.

Exercise D: Fill in the chart with the derivatives of the given adjectives or adverbs. Then, provide one **synonym** and one **antonym**, taking into account their meaning in the specific text above.

	Verb	Noun	Adjective	Adverb
1.	exclude	exclusion	exclusive	exclusively
2.	succeed	success	successful	successfully
3.	last	–	lasting	lastingly
4.	socialize	socialization/society	social	socially

		Synonym	Antonym
1.	exclusively	solely	unrestrictedly
2.	successful	competent	unsuccessful
3.	lasting	continuous	temporary
4.	social	collective	unsocial

Exercise E: Write 4 sentences using the following words: temporary, unsocial, unrestricted, unsuccessful. You must write 1 sentence for each of these words. Use between 8 and 15 words in each sentence.

(Suggested Answers)

1. This measure is only temporary and will be lifted soon.
2. He is described as an unsocial person by his peers.
3. Research cannot make use of personal data unrestrictedly.
4. His attempts to follow the course were unsuccessful.

Debate 3

Online Education

Paragraph 7

A Online education has become a visible trend in contemporary times. In fact, students may well one day learn exclusively from their home-based computers instead of attending traditional schools in person. **B** <u>Of course, there has been some successful learning accomplished through this form of learning, such as with English-language lessons, whereby students and teachers use online chats, Skype and accompanying headsets to facilitate communication and education.</u> **C** At the same time, the advantages of traditional forms of education far **exceed** those of online methods. Students acquire social and life skills that cannot be achieved through simple online lessons. They are able to connect and learn from in-person classmates and teachers that enrich their lives with lasting relationships and guidance. **D**

Reading Comprehension

1. The word **exceed** in §7 is closest in meaning to
   a. underestimate.　　　　c. estimate.
   b. transcend.　　　　　　d. shrink.

2. Based on the text, the author concludes that
   a. online education will soon replace traditional classrooms.
   b. traditional classrooms need to be reformulated for the digital era.
   c. traditional classrooms are still superior to online platforms.
   d. online education remains the standard for students to develop socially.

3. What does the author think may occur in the future with student learning?
   a. Online learning will be abandoned as a mode of education.
   b. Students may receive their education exclusively at-home through a computer.
   c. Teachers will teach students in-person and through the Internet.
   d. Parents will force teachers to provide extra classes online through Skype.

4. Which sentence below best expresses the essential information in the underlined sentence in §7?
   a. Online education has been a failure overall in teaching students.
   b. Online education has been effective only with teaching math and science.
   c. Online education has been successful to a degree in enhancing learning.
   d. Online education has been a platform only embraced by engineering students.

5. All of the following are attributes of online education **EXCEPT**
   a. success in teaching languages.
   b. effective use of audio/visual technology.
   c. teaching through digital applications.
   d. higher standardized test scores.

6. Look at the four squares, **A**, **B**, **C** and **D**, which indicate where the following sentence could be added to the passage. Where would the sentence best fit?　Right Answer: C

   Employing these forms of technology has made learning more dynamic and interactive.

7. Select the appropriate sentences from the answer choices and match them to attributes of each form of learning. **TWO** of the answer choices will **NOT** be used. **This question is worth 3 points.**

   a. Students form life-long bonds with teachers and peers.
   b. Teachers make use of technologies like video conference.
   c. Parents are forced to compromise some of their moral values in the process.
   d. Students have little ability to tailor their learning needs.
   e. Teachers use digital applications to communicate with students.
   f. Students receive mentoring opportunities to bolster their career and life paths.
   g. Teachers are able to reach students all over the world to convey lessons seamlessly.

Online Learning:	B/E/G
Traditional Classroom Learning:	A/F

Debate 3

Online Education is Becoming Important

Paragraph 1

Online learning, namely because of the technological **innovations** in broadband video service, has become a more **effective** means of teaching. The question remains, though, whether it has developed to a point to **replace** traditional university education, particularly in light of the ever **increasing** costs of college **tuition** and the subsequent crisis in student loans in the United States. According to government agencies, there are nearly $1 trillion spent in outstanding student loans across the country. Given this financial **burden**, it's reasonable to wonder whether the extra income those with a college degree earn actually **outweighs** the cost of repaying the loans needed to receive the education. Thus, it may well be that online education will serve as the solution to this dilemma because of its affordability and quality.

Paragraph 2

Online educational institutions have existed for years now. One in **particular**, Khan Academy, has established itself as a **leading provider** of educational lessons. The company endeavors to give a free top-tier education to users anywhere in the world. Since its **inception**, Khan's YouTube channel has generated hundreds of millions of views. In contrast, a **prestigious** Ivy League institution has generated only around 75 million **views**. Moreover, this school only has half of the millions of subscribers that Khan features. This comparison underscores the **efficacy** of video and online learning. At the same time, these online **outlets** do not offer the **accredited** degree that so many employers desire from their future employees. Most companies do not accept coursework in **lieu** of an **actual** accredited undergraduate or graduate degree.

Paragraph 3

This, I believe, is where the change must **occur**. For instance, iTunes University offers almost every single class one can take at a prestigious Ivy-League university. Yet, because students don't pay any **form** of tuition there, a student doesn't receive any type of accreditation of value in the job market. This is where many companies are going wrong. Many current employees, for example, take job-related classes. The **certification** they receive for it is not important compared to the actual **knowledge** they **accumulate**. Most employers, after a candidate has established a strong work **track** record, care less about where job seekers went to college and more about what they can actually do on a job.

Paragraph 4

The online world democratizes all information making it available to the masses. Students around the world have access to leading experts and thinkers regardless of their physical location. If I'm going to go into massive debt to finance an education, I want to make sure I get only the very best instruction possible. With an online platform, moreover, students can go at their own **pace** tailoring the **experience** to their needs. This **flexibility** is especially attractive to mid-career professionals in their 40s or 50s who are looking to retool and transition into a new career. It is highly unlikely they would be able to repay a fresh six-figure loan in their **lifetime** and see a marked **improvement** in their lifestyle.

Paragraph 5

The traditional college degree is becoming less and less **relevant** in our digital age abounding with constant change and new innovation. The value of it, furthermore, seems ludicrous when **contextualized** in the achievements of **prominent entrepreneurs**, like Steve Jobs who dropped out of college. Upon dropping out of school, Jobs began to audit classes at no cost, thereby building an education around the **subject** matters that he believed would serve him best in his fields of interest. Ironically, the Apple Computer **employment** page reads that "Apple is a place where students and college graduates **thrive**." but doesn't mention much about self-motivated people who don't have a traditional university degree.

Paragraph 6

For those with the money to attend a traditional college, there may be some value still in going to school. For those, though, who would have to **borrow** hundreds of thousands of dollars, I recommend going online to get the knowledge you need without having to **cripple** yourself financially for potentially your whole life. Take your **cue** from great minds like Steve Jobs and look to acquire the skills that help you establish in the field **endeavor** of your choosing. Don't fall into the debt **trap** and keep your mind open to opportunities and ways of making a living that embraces the **unconventional** and your imagination. Online education, **ultimately**, may not be an alternative solution to learning but the new standard for those looking to change the world.

Vocabulary Building

Exercise A: Choose the option (**a**, **b**, **c** or **d**) which fits best each sentence.

1. Many students fall into a debt .... and find themselves unable to pay off their debts.
   - **a.** endeavor
   - **b.** flexibility
   - **c. trap**
   - **d.** employment

2. When he started working consistently, there was a(n) .... in his class performance.
   - **a. improvement**
   - **b.** view
   - **c.** experience
   - **d.** knowledge

3. Online courses allow students to work at their own ....
   - **a.** track
   - **b. pace**
   - **c.** provider
   - **d.** form

4. Dyslexic students can sit for oral exams in .... of written ones.
   - **a.** particular
   - **b.** cue
   - **c.** lifetime
   - **d. lieu**

5. A large number of schools cannot meet the .... cost of electronic equipment.
   - **a.** effective
   - **b.** relevant
   - **c.** leading
   - **d. increasing**

6. The professor is a(n) .... member of the academic community with many publications and presentations.
   - **a.** accredited
   - **b. prominent**
   - **c.** subject
   - **d.** actual

Exercise B: Fill in the blanks in the following sentences using words from the box. You may need to change the word. There are 2 extra words in the box you do not need to use.

a. thrive	**b.** contextualize	**c.** borrow	**d.** occur	**e.** accumulate	**f.** cripple	**g.** outweigh	**h.** replace

1. The teacher ..contextualized.. the lesson by telling his students a story.
2. The sales of English books ....thrive...... in China with millions of orders placed every year.
3. There is no point in ..accumulating... knowledge if you cannot use it effectively.
4. Despite the changes that .....occurred......, there were no signs of progress.
5. The advantages of online education .....outweigh..... the disadvantages.
6. The strike ......crippled...... the university and all lectures and services were temporarily suspended.

Exercise C: Fill in the definitions using words from the box below. There are 2 extra words in the box that you do not need to use.

a. burden	**b.** inception	**c.** innovation	**d.** certification	**e.** tuition	**f.** outlet	**g.** efficacy	**h.** entrepreneur

1. ......Burden...... is the strain, usually financial, or the pressure imposed on a person.
2. ....Certification.... means the proof of a specific level of attainment.
3. .....Innovation..... refers to a major change implemented on a procedure.
4. ...Entrepreneur... is a businessman who launches a company in a new business field.
5. ......Efficacy...... means the ability to do something competently.
6. ......Tuition...... is a form of instruction or teaching.

Exercise D: Fill in the chart with the derivatives of the given adjectives or adverbs. Then, provide one **synonym** and one **antonym**, taking into account their meaning in the specific text above.

	Verb	**Noun**	**Adjective**	**Adverb**
1.	–	ultimatum	ultimate	ultimately
2.	lead	leader(ship)	leading	leadingly
3.	increase	increase	increasing	increasingly
4.	convene	convention	unconventional	unconventionally
5.	–	prestige	prestigious	prestigiously
6.	relate	relevance	relevant	relevantly

		Synonym	**Antonym**
1.	ultimately	finally	primarily
2.	leading	top	average
3.	increasing	rising	decreasing
4.	unconventional	innovative	conventional
5.	prestigious	respectable	infamous
6.	relevant	applicable	irrelevant

Exercise E: Write 6 sentences using the following words: primarily, irrelevant, average, infamous, decreasing, conventional. You must write 1 sentence for each of these words. Use between 8 and 15 words in each sentence.

(Suggested Answers)

1. He is primarily concerned about the safety of his students who surf the Internet.
2. Your essay is irrelevant to the topic you were assigned.
3. Her average marks won't help her when she applies to university.
4. The infamous robber was arrested yesterday after months of police investigation.
5. The decreasing number of students attending classes is worrying.
6. Most teachers employ conventional methods of instruction.

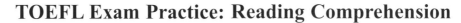

TOEFL Exam Practice: Reading Comprehension

Paragraph 1

Online learning, namely because of the technological innovations in broadband video service, has become a more effective means of teaching. The question remains, though, whether it has developed to a point to replace traditional university education, particularly in light of the ever increasing costs of college tuition and the subsequent crisis in student loans in the United States. According to government agencies, there are nearly $1 trillion in outstanding student loans across the country. Given this financial burden, it's reasonable to wonder whether the extra income those with a college degree earn actually **outweighs** the cost of repaying the loans needed to receive the education. Thus, it may well be that online education will serve as the solution to this dilemma because of its affordability and quality.

1. The word **outweighs** in §1 is closest in meaning to
   a. diminishes.
   b. rekindles.
   c. holds more value.
   d. retains less mass.

2. According to the text, why does the author question the value of a traditional college degree?
   a. He thinks the cost is too low for one.
   b. He believes employers don't value it.
   c. He wonders whether online education has staying power.
   d. He doubts the financial incentive for earning one.

Paragraph 2

Online educational institutions have existed for years now. One in particular, Khan Academy, has established itself as a leading provider of educational lessons. The company endeavors to give a free top-tier education to users anywhere in the world. Since its inception, Khan's YouTube channel has generated hundreds of millions of views. In contrast, a prestigious Ivy League institution has generated only around 75 million views. Moreover, this school only has half of the millions of subscribers that Khan features. This comparison underscores the **efficacy** of video and online learning. At the same time, these online outlets do not offer the accredited degree that so many employers desire from their future employees. Most companies do not accept coursework **in lieu of** an actual accredited undergraduate or graduate degree.

3. Why does the author discuss the work of Khan Academy in his argument?
   a. to underscore the value of traditional college degrees
   b. to illustrate the effectiveness and power of online learning
   c. to show why more colleges need to abandon online learning
   d. to show why the Ivy-League has been undervalued in the job market

4. The word **efficacy** in §2 is closest in meaning to
   a. failure.   c. persuasiveness.
   b. effectiveness.   d. graduation.

5. The expression **in lieu of** in §2 is closest in meaning to
   a. instead of.   c. since.
   b. despite.   d. contrastingly.

Paragraph 3

This, I believe, is where the change must occur. For instance, iTunes University offers almost every single class one can take at a prestigious Ivy-League university. Yet, because students don't pay any form of tuition there, a student doesn't receive any type of accreditation of value in the job market. This is where many companies are going wrong. Many current employees, for example, take job-related classes. The certification they receive for it is not important compared to the actual knowledge they **accumulate**. Most employers, after a candidate has established a strong work track record, care less about where job seekers went to college and more about what they can actually do on a job.

6. What does the writer think companies should do when evaluating job candidates?
   a. place less value on paid education
   b. place more value on skill acquisition than educational degree
   c. place less value on online educational platforms
   d. place the ultimate value on whether a student attended an Ivy-League education

7. The word **accumulate** in §3 is closest in meaning to
   a. diminish.
   b. relinquish.
   c. erode.
   d. gather.

Paragraph 4

The online world democratizes all information making it available to the masses. Students around the world have access to leading experts and thinkers regardless of their physical location. If I'm going to go into massive debt to finance an education, I want to make sure I get only the very best instruction possible. With an online platform, **moreover**, students can go at their own pace tailoring the experience to their needs. This flexibility is especially attractive to mid-career professionals in their 40s or 50s who are looking to retool and transition into a new career. It is highly unlikely they would be able to repay a fresh six-figure loan in their lifetime and see a marked improvement in their lifestyle.

8. Based on §4, the author argues for online education
 a. because it costs less and is more flexible.
 b. because it takes longer than traditional college education.
 c. because teachers in online platforms are superior.
 d. because middle-age students find them disadvantageous.

9. The word **moreover** in §4 is closest in meaning to
 a. in contrast.
 b. in addition.
 c. despite.
 d. in fact.

Paragraph 5

The traditional college degree is becoming less and less relevant in our digital age abounding with constant change and new innovation. The value of it, furthermore, seems **ludicrous** when contextualized in the achievements of prominent entrepreneurs like Steve Jobs who dropped out of college. Upon dropping out of school, Jobs began to audit classes at no cost, thereby building an education around the subject matters that he believed would serve him best in his fields of interest. Ironically, the Apple Computer employment page reads that "Apple is a place where students and college graduates thrive." but doesn't mention much about self-motivated people who don't have a traditional university degree.

---

10. All of the following are characteristics of Steve Jobs **EXCEPT**
 a. college drop-out.   c. technologically savvy.
 b. innovative mind.   d. conventional thinker.

 c. believes Steve Jobs would have no problem becoming an engineering teacher at a college.
 d. argues Steve Jobs would have been better off with a traditional college education.

11. It can be inferred that the writer
 a. thinks Steve Jobs would easily rise at the ranks of Apple.
 b. contends Steve Jobs would have difficulty getting a job at Apple.

12. The word **ludicrous** in §5 is closest in meaning to
 a. sound.
 b. stupendous.
 c. ridiculous.
 d. believable.

Paragraph 6

A For those with the money to attend a traditional college, there may be some value still in going to school. For those, though, who would have to borrow hundreds of thousands of dollars, I recommend going online to get the knowledge you need without having to cripple yourself financially for potentially your whole life. **B** Take your cue from great minds like Steve Jobs and look to acquire the skills that help you establish in the field endeavor of your choosing. Don't fall into the debt trap and keep your mind open to opportunities and ways of making a living that **embraces** the unconventional and your imagination. **C** Online education, ultimately, may not be an alternative solution to learning but the new standard for those looking to change the world. **D**

---

13. The word **embraces** in §6 is closest in meaning to
 a. denies.   c. hides.
 b. satisfies.   d. values.

14. Look at the four squares, **A**, **B**, **C** and **D**, which indicate where the following sentence could be added to the passage. Where would the sentence best fit?   Right Answer: B

There have been a bevy of highly successful people who never received a college degree.

Paragraphs 1 to 6

15. An introductory sentence for a brief summary of the passage is provided below. Complete the summary by selecting the **THREE** answer choices that express the most important ideas in the passage. Some sentences do not belong in the summary because they express ideas that are not presented in the passage or are ideas of minor importance. **This question is worth 2 points.**

Compared to traditional forms of learning, online education forms provide students with a sound education at an attractive price.

 a. Middle-aged students benefit from online educational platforms, especially financially.
 b. The cost of traditional college is falling because of the emergence of online platforms.
 c. Online education enables professors and students to connect from various parts of the world.
 d. Online learning portals make it easy for students to flexibly tailor their education to their needs.
 e. Companies embrace only unconventional, self-motivated employees.

Debate 3

Wearing Uniforms In Schools

Paragraph 1

I can see the many arguments why students should or should not have to wear **uniforms**. But, for me, one of the major **reasons** we shouldn't have to wear them is because it helps us **build** our **confidence**. It's harder to feel confident while wearing a uniform. They often **cause distractions** during the day, believe it or not. I know some people think they **create unity** and so forth, but this is at the **cost** of feeling empowered. Schools, instead, should **implement** simple clothing **guidelines** instead of uniforms so that we know what we can and cannot wear. School is supposed to teach us to be **strong** and **develop** our own **judgment**. I don't see how telling us exactly what we have to wear is teaching us anything. Furthermore, letting us follow a **set** of guidelines will help us in our **careers**, where our **attire** won't be **completely dictated** to us. Each **employer** will have a set of guidelines for us to follow **individually**. With a different **approach** to school **dress**, students will get back their confidence and be more prepared in life.

Vocabulary Building

Exercise A: Choose the option (**a**, **b**, **c** or **d**) which fits best each sentence.

1. You cannot allow a free dress code at the .... of poorer students.

   a. cost
   b. reason
   c. uniform
   d. career

2. All students follow a(n) .... of rules at school.

   a. approach
   b. set
   c. dress
   d. guideline

Exercise B: Fill in the blanks in the following sentences using words from the box below. There are 2 extra words in the box you do not need to use. You cannot change the words.

a. develop	b. dictate	c. build	d. cause	e. implement	f. create

1. A teacher should not ......dictate...... to her students what they should do.
2. Students need to ......develop......... skills such as creativity and communication.
3. The lead teacher decided to ......implement..... new stricter rules.
4. All the activities will help learners to ......build.......... more confidence.

Exercise C: Fill in the definitions using words from the box below. There are 2 extra words in the box that you do not need to use.

a. attire	b. unity	c. judgment	d. distraction	e. confidence	f. employer

1. ......Judgement...... is one's critical thinking ability.
2. ......Attire...... is a formal word used for clothes.
3. ......Distraction...... refers to diverting one's attention.
4. ......Confidence...... is the quality of believing in yourself.

Exercise D: Fill in the chart with the derivatives of the given adjectives or adverbs. Then, provide one **synonym** and one **antonym**, taking into account their meaning in the specific text above.

	Verb	Noun	Adjective	Adverb
1.	strengthen	strength	strong	strongly
2.	complete	completion	complete	completely
3.	individualize	individual	individual	individually
4.	-	exactness	exact	exactly

		Synonym	Antonym
1.	strong	powerful	weak
2.	completely	entirely	partially
3.	individually	personally	collectively
4.	exactly	precisely	vaguely

Exercise E: Write 4 sentences using the following words: partially, collectively, weak, vaguely. You must write 1 sentence for each of these words. Use between 8 and 15 words in each sentence.   (Suggested Answers)

1. The topic was covered partially by the press.
2. The parents worked collectively and managed to persuade the head teacher.
3. He is still weak, as he is recovering from his accident.
4. She answered vaguely, avoiding to express her views openly.

Wearing Uniforms In Schools

Paragraph 1

A I can see the many arguments why students should or should not have to wear uniforms. But, for me, one of the major reasons we shouldn't have to wear them is because it helps us build our confidence. **B** It's harder to feel confident while wearing a uniform. They often cause distractions during the day, believe it or not. I know some people think they create unity and so forth, but this is at the cost of feeling **empowered**. Schools, instead, should implement simple clothing guidelines instead of uniforms so that we know what we can and cannot wear. **C** School is supposed to teach us to be strong and develop our own judgment. I don't see how telling us exactly what we have to wear is teaching us anything. Furthermore, letting us follow a set of guidelines will help us in our careers, where our attire won't be completely dictated to us. Each employer will have a set of guidelines for us to follow individually. With a different approach to school dress, students will get back their confidence and be more prepared in life. **D**

Reading Comprehension

1. The word **empowered** in §1 is closest in meaning to
   a. weakened.   **c.** dependent.
   b. confident.   **d.** belittled.

2. Based on the text, why does the author think students shouldn't wear uniforms?
   a. They make students feel inferior to their teachers.
   b. They make students feel less independent.
   c. They make students feel stronger in their own identity.
   d. They make students feel smarter than their peers.

3. What is the benefit of not having uniforms in terms of professional life?
   a. Students develop their own judgment in deciding what to wear.
   b. Students learn how to break the rules when dressing for their job.
   c. Students discover the tastes of their teachers and parents in terms of dress.
   d. Students decide what is best for them not to wear during the school year.

4. Which sentence below best expresses the essential information in the underlined sentence in §1?
   a. A more rigid uniform policy is beneficial for students in the professional world.
   b. A more flexible uniform policy hurts students in the professional world.
   c. A more flexible uniform policy strengthens students in the professional world.
   d. A more rigid uniform policy curtails the ability of a student to conform in the professional world.

5. All of the following are traits developed by not having a strict uniform policy **EXCEPT**
   a. good judgment.
   b. confidence.
   c. group think.
   d. personal expression.

6. Look at the four squares, **A**, **B**, **C** and **D**, which indicate where the following sentence could be added to the passage. Where would the sentence best fit?   Right Answer: D

   Ultimately, it would be foolish to hinder students from growing into independent adults all because of a silly uniform.

7. An introductory sentence for a brief summary of the passage is provided below. Complete the summary by selecting the **THREE** answer choices that express the most important ideas in the passage. Some sentences do not belong in the summary because they express ideas that are not presented in the passage or are ideas of minor importance. **This question is worth 2 points.**

   A strict school uniform policy doesn't help students develop their own judgment and confidence.

   a. In their professional lives, students will have to make good decisions about how they dress.
   b. Students have demonstrated a preference for rigid uniform policies in school.
   c. Students will never learn to think for themselves if they are constantly told what to do.
   d. Teachers think that policing school uniform violations is a good use of time in the classroom.
   e. Being told what to wear at school will not help students develop a strong sense of self to excel in life.

Wearing Uniforms In Schools

Paragraph 2

Like with confidence, we should **assert** our own unique **individuality** and **expressive personality** in school and later in our professional lives. It's hard to be a unique **person** when we all have to dress the same. Our teachers always tell us to be ourselves and not pay **attention** to what other people say and **think** and yet we are asked to **conform** in **terms** of what we wear. **Uniforms erode** our **ability** to **express** our own personality and unique **perspective** on life. Being **different** and **establishing** our own **identity** is what education **encourages** us to do, not to be simple robots who talk, dress and act the same. **Creating** a school dress **policy** that is more **flexible** to let your special personality **shine** is a great way for us to **develop** more as young adults.

Vocabulary Building

Exercise A: Choose the option (**a**, **b**, **c** or **d**) which fits best each sentence.

1. Silk clothes are considered to be the best in .... of quality.
   - **a.** person
   - **b.** attention
   - **c.** terms
   - **d.** uniforms

2. You should .... your own identity as a designer.
   - **a.** encourage
   - **b.** think
   - **c.** establish
   - **d.** shine

Exercise B: Fill in the blanks in the following sentences using words from the box below. There are 2 extra words in the box you do not need to use. You cannot change the words.

| **a.** create | **b.** develop | **c.** express | **d.** assert | **e.** conform | **f.** erode |

1. It is best to .....conform..... to the dress etiquette of the company.
2. You should .....assert..... your right to speak for yourself.
3. Fame and riches can easily .....erode..... family values.
4. People often .....express..... their personality by wearing eccentric clothes.

Exercise C: Fill in the definitions using words from the box below. There are 2 extra words in the box that you do not need to use.

| **a.** policy | **b.** attention | **c.** personality | **d.** ability | **e.** perspective | **f.** identity |

1. .....Perspective..... is the way one looks at a situation.
2. .....Personality..... refers to the traits of a person.
3. .....Identity..... means what makes one person distinct from another.
4. .....Policy..... refers to the course of action taken to deal with an issue.

Exercise D: Fill in the chart with the derivatives of the given adjectives or adverbs. Then, provide one **synonym** and one **antonym**, taking into account their meaning in the specific text above.

	Verb	Noun	Adjective	Adverb
1.	flex	flexibility	flexible	flexibly
2.	differ	difference	different	differently
3.	express	expression	expressive	expressively
4.	simplify	simplicity/ simplification	simple	simply

		Synonym	Antonym
1.	flexible	adaptable	rigid
2.	different	diverse	same
3.	expressive	communicative	inexpressive
4.	simple	mere	sophisticated

Exercise E: Write 4 sentences using the following words: sophisticated, rigid, same, inexpressive. You must write 1 sentence for each of these words. Use between 8 and 15 words in each sentence. (Suggested Answers)

1. His manners are too sophisticated for my taste.
2. He adopted a rigid policy which caused many objections.
3. You should not wear the same clothes every day.
4. His face was completely inexpressive despite the pressure.

Debate 4

Wearing Uniforms In Schools

Paragraph 2

A Like with confidence, we should assert our own unique individuality and **expressive** personality in school and later in our professional lives. **B** It's hard to be a unique person when we all have to dress the same. **C** <u>Our teachers always tell us to be ourselves and not pay attention to what other people say and think and yet we are asked to conform in terms of what we wear.</u> Uniforms **erode** our ability to express our own personality and unique perspective on life. Being different and establishing our own identity is what education encourages us to do, not to be simple robots who talk, dress and act the same. Creating a school dress policy that is more flexible to let your special personality shine is a great way for us to develop more as young adults. **D**

Reading Comprehension

1. The word **erode** in §2 is closest in meaning to
   a. embolden.
   b. strengthen.
   c. neutralize.
   d. weaken.

2. According to the text, what characteristic is the author seeking by eliminating uniforms?
   a. conformity
   b. individuality
   c. cohesion
   d. reserve

3. Based on the style in the passage, one can infer that the author is a(n)
   a. student.
   b. parent.
   c. administrator.
   d. teacher.

4. Which sentence below best expresses the essential information in the underlined sentence in §2?
   a. There is consistency between the uniform policy and classroom instruction.
   b. The school uniform policy parallels the values taught by teachers.
   c. The school uniform policy seems at odds with the lessons taught by instructors.
   d. There is little for teachers to control or learn from the school uniform policy.

5. Which of the following is **NOT** one of the characteristics of a unique personality?
   a. expressiveness
   b. perspective
   c. identity
   d. likeness

6. Look at the four squares, **A**, **B**, **C** and **D**, which indicate where the following sentence could be added to the passage. Where would the sentence best fit?   Right Answer: B

> *Apparently, there seems to be a contradiction between what schools say they want to teach and what uniforms imply.*

7. An introductory sentence for a brief summary of the passage is provided below. Complete the summary by selecting the **THREE** answer choices that express the most important ideas in the passage. Some sentences do not belong in the summary because they express ideas that are not presented in the passage or are ideas of minor importance. **This question is worth 2 points.**

> *Making students wear school uniforms hurts their ability to develop their own unique personality.*

   a. There is a discrepancy between what schools say they want to teach and what they practice.
   b. Letting students pick and wear what they want helps them be themselves.
   c. Teachers believe uniforms are essential for students to focus in school.
   d. Parents think that school uniforms are too expensive to pay for every year.
   e. School uniforms cut against the very value of personality and individuality that schools claim they want to instil.

Debate 4

Wearing Uniforms In Schools

Paragraph 3

Students have enough stress in their lives and worrying about uniforms is just another **layer** of discomfort. Shouldn't we be trying to make student life easier not harder? Uniforms are a **burden** during the school day because of all of the rules and **regulations** around them. Teachers and administrators are always **nagging** you about having your shirt **tail tucked**-in and making sure you are wearing the right kind of shoes. It takes away from our **ability** to **focus** on our studies and prepare for tests. **Moreover**, if you **violate** the dress **code** too many times, you have to worry about **detention** and other **forms** of **punishment**. I sometimes am more concerned about my uniform than whether I am going to the right class or have prepared well enough for an important test. This always plays into our confidence building **like** I **mentioned** above. Some students, though, feel self-**conscious** and confident about their appearance in the school's uniform. But this **distracts** their focus from course work and learning, too. **By** letting students wear what they feel comfortable in, **as long as** it is not **offensive**, helps them to be **completely invested** in their education.

Vocabulary Building

Exercise A: Choose the option (**a**, **b**, **c** or **d**) which fits best each sentence.

1. .... you said, uniforms can demotivate students.
   a. Like
   b. Moreover
   c. By
   d. As long as

2. There are many .... of punishment to discipline someone.
   a. abilities
   b. forms
   c. codes
   d. tails

Exercise B: Fill in the blanks in the following sentences using the correct form of the words from the box below. There are 2 extra words in the box you do not need to use.

a. nag	b. tuck	c. violate	d. distract	e. invest	f. mention

1. Stop ......nagging...... all day long about the new working hours.
2. Remain silent or else you ...will distract... your classmates.
3. She ......violated...... the school rules and will have to face the consequences.
4. He ......invests....... a lot of his time in helping the poor.

Exercise C: Fill in the definitions using words from the box below. There are 2 extra words in the box that you do not need to use.

a. focus	b. detention	c. punishment	d. burden	e. layer	f. regulation

1. ......Regulation...... refers to a set of rules defining a code of conduct.
2. ......Layer...... means metaphorically a level.
3. ......Detention...... is the punishment of being kept at school after lessons are over.
4. ......Focus...... is the point one concentrates on.

Exercise D: Fill in the chart with the derivatives of the given adjectives or adverbs. Then, provide one **synonym** and one **antonym**, taking into account their meaning in the specific text above.

	Verb	Noun	Adjective	Adverb
1.	offend	offence	offensive	offensively
2.	complete	completion	complete	completely
3.	-	conscience/ consciousness	conscious	consciously
4.	confide	confidence	confident	confidently

		Synonym	Antonym
1.	offensive	provocative	inoffensive
2.	completely	entirely	partially
3.	conscious	aware	unaware
4.	confident	assertive	non-assertive

Exercise E: Write 4 sentences using the following words: partially, non-assertive, inoffensive, unaware. You must write 1 sentence for each of these words. Use between 8 and 15 words in each sentence.

(Suggested Answers)

1. You are partially right in your claims about uniforms.
2. His non-assertive manners did not persuade the manager.
3. They adopted a low-profile inoffensive behavior to approach him.
4. He was blissfully unaware until he received a phone call from the police.

Wearing Uniforms In Schools

Paragraph 3

A Students have enough stress in their lives and worrying about uniforms is just another layer of discomfort. Shouldn't we be trying to make student life easier not harder? Uniforms are a burden during the school day because of all of the rules and regulations around them. **B** Teachers and administrators are always **nagging** you about having your shirt tail tucked-in and making sure you are wearing the right kind of shoes. It takes away from our ability to focus on our studies and prepare for tests. Moreover, if you violate the dress code too many times, you have to worry about detention and other forms of punishment. **C** I sometimes am more concerned about my uniform than whether I am going to the right class or have prepared well enough for an important test. This always plays into our confidence building like I mentioned above. Some students, though, feel self-conscious and confident about their appearance in the school's uniform. But this distracts their focus from course work and learning, too. By letting students wear what they feel comfortable in, as long as it is not offensive, helps them to be completely invested in their education. **D**

Reading Comprehension

1. The word **nagging** in §3 is closest in meaning to
   a. complimenting.
   c. stressing.
   b. bothering.
   d. interrupting.

2. Based on the text, what is the writer's primary argument against uniforms?
   a. They make it easier for students to focus on their studies.
   b. They make it harder for students to be distracted from their schoolwork.
   c. They make it harder for students to focus on their courses in school.
   d. They make it easier for students to cheat on exams for their classes.

3. Why does the writer ask a rhetoric question in the passage?
   a. to distract the reader from the subject matter being addressed
   b. to try and make her viewpoint more difficult to comprehend
   c. to question the arguments for not letting students wear uniforms at school
   d. to add an element of style to her piece, making it more engaging

4. Which sentence below best expresses the essential information in the underlined sentence in §3?
   a. Uniforms cause stress that distracts students from their classwork.
   b. Uniforms make it easier for students to focus on their test preparation.
   c. Uniforms have little impact on students' ability to get to class on-time.
   d. Uniforms are helping students to attend school more regularly.

5. All of the following describe the relationship between uniforms and student performance **EXCEPT**
   a. students are less focused on studies.
   b. teachers are more confident.
   c. students worry too much about rules.
   d. teachers trouble students about their appearance.

6. Look at the four squares, **A**, **B**, **C** and **D**, which indicate where the following sentence could be added to the passage. Where would the sentence best fit?   Right Answer: A

   Schools seem to be striving to put more obstacles up for students to overcome in order to achieve.

7. Select the appropriate sentences from the answer choices and match them to the relationship between school uniforms and student stress levels. **TWO** of the answer choices will **NOT** be used. **This question is worth 3 points.**

   a. Students have to think about punishments like detention for uniform violations.
   b. Teachers don't care what students are wearing despite the rules about wearing uniforms.
   c. Without strict uniform policies, students could have more focus on their courses.
   d. Most students find what teachers wear to school offensive.
   e. Students would believe in themselves a bit more by making good decisions about what they wear.
   f. Teachers are always bothering students about not following the school uniform rules.
   g. The school uniform makes some students uncomfortable about their appearance in them.

Creates Stress for Students:	A/F/G
Lessens Stress for Students:	C/E

Wearing Uniforms In Schools

Paragraph 4

By letting students **exercise** their own judgment **with** regard to what they wear to school, schools **enable** them to become more **accountable** for their lives. Some people might **argue** that young people need **structure** and **direction**, but I think **after** a **certain** age, students are able to think **for** themselves and take **ownership** of their lives. Being told all the time, what to wear, how to think, what to eat, when to come, when to go, wears **on** a young person's ability to be an **independent** human being. School is supposed to help us learn **personal discretion** and life skills that go **beyond** the classrooms. I don't think we're really learning anything if we are always being told what to do without having a say **in** our **actions**. What are we really learning except for perhaps how to **follow** directions? Is school preparing us for life or the army? I think **eliminating** school uniforms will be a huge **step** in letting students begin to **develop** their own judgment skills.

Vocabulary Building

Exercise A: Choose the option (**a**, **b**, **c** or **d**) which fits best each sentence.

1. Many articles have been written .... regard to bullying.

   a. on   **c.** by

   b. at   **d. with**

2. You clearly went .... what was required of you.

   a. beyond   **c.** for

   b. over   **d.** in

Exercise B: Fill in the blanks in the following sentences using the correct form of the words from the box below. There are 2 extra words in the box you do not need to use.

a. enable	**b.** eliminate	**c.** exercise	**d.** argue	**e.** follow	**f.** develop

1. Many learners are in need of ......developing...... their communication skills.
2. He ......followed...... the directions and found his way out of the old city.
3. ......Eliminating...... school uniforms will not solve behavior problems.
4. The new policy ......enabled...... weaker students to join a class of their choice.

Exercise C: Fill in the definitions using words from the box below. There are 2 extra words in the box that you do not need to use.

a. ownership	**b.** discretion	**c.** structure	**d.** action	**e.** direction	**f.** step

1. ......Discretion...... is the power to act using one's own judgment.
2. ......Structure...... is a construction or framework.
3. ......Ownership...... means possession of a thing.
4. ......Action...... refers to something done or accomplished.

Exercise D: Fill in the chart with the derivatives of the given adjectives or adverbs. Then, provide one **synonym** and one **antonym**, taking into account their meaning in the specific text above.

	Verb	Noun	Adjective	Adverb
1.	-	certainty	certain	certainly
2.	depend	(in)dependence	independent	independently
3.	personalize	personality/ personalization	personal	personally
4.	account	accountability	accountable	accountably

		Synonym	Antonym
1.	certain	sure	uncertain
2.	independent	free	dependent
3.	personal	own	impersonal
4.	accountable	responsible	irresponsible

Exercise E: Write 4 sentences using the following words: dependent, impersonal, uncertain, irresponsible. You must write 1 sentence for each of these words. Use between 8 and 15 words in each sentence.

(Suggested Answers)

1. In the past acquiring knowledge was mainly dependent on books.
2. His teaching style was completely impersonal and tended to ignore students' needs.
3. The future of the project seems uncertain as more and more problems arise.
4. His behavior was totally irresponsible at the day of the meeting.

Wearing Uniforms In Schools

Paragraph 4

A By letting students **exercise** their own judgment with regard to what they wear to school, schools enable them to become more accountable for their lives. Some people might argue that young people need structure and direction, but I think after a certain age, students are able to think for themselves and take ownership of their lives. **B** Being told all the time, what to wear, how to think, what to eat, when to come, when to go, wears on a young person's ability to be an independent human being. School is supposed to help us learn personal discretion and life skills that go beyond the classrooms. I don't think we're really learning anything if we are always being told what to do without having a say in our actions. **C** What are we really learning except for perhaps how to follow directions? Is school preparing us for life or the army? I think eliminating school uniforms will be a huge step in letting students begin to develop their own judgment skills. **D**

Reading Comprehension

1. The word **exercise** in §4 is closest in meaning to
   a. work out.
   b. fear.
   c. regress.
   d. use.

2. Based on the text, what characteristic does the author believe students develop by not having to wear uniforms?
   a. conformity
   b. co-dependence
   c. responsible independence
   d. risk management

3. What role does the writer think school lessons should serve in a student's life?
   a. They should be limited to classroom instruction.
   b. They should transcend what is taught simply in course books.
   c. They should only reinforce the values parents teach students at home.
   d. They should stress the acquisition of foreign language skills over science.

4. Which sentence below best expresses the essential information in the underlined sentence in §4?
   a. Contrary to popular thought, students need less rigidity and more flexibility to develop.
   b. Schools should stress fixed lessons and rules over fluid lessons.
   c. Teachers must observe strict guidelines when enforcing uniform codes.
   d. Parents need to cooperate with teachers in developing a fixed uniform policy.

5. All of the following are reasons the writer is against school uniforms **EXCEPT**
   a. student judgment.
   b. student personality.
   c. student conformity.
   d. student individuality.

6. Look at the four squares, **A**, **B**, **C** and **D**, which indicate where the following sentence could be added to the passage. Where would the sentence best fit?   Right Answer: D

   With these abilities, students will be able to reach their full potential as citizens.

7. An introductory sentence for a brief summary of the passage is provided below. Complete the summary by selecting the **THREE** answer choices that express the most important ideas in the passage. Some sentences do not belong in the summary because they express ideas that are not presented in the passage or are ideas of minor importance. **This question is worth 2 points.**

   Students become more independent and develop sound judgment
   for the rest of their lives by not having to wear uniforms.

   a. School should have a strict set of rules and regulations for students to follow.
   b. Uniform policies make students simple-minded and lacking confidence.
   c. In the workforce, people wear whatever they want to.
   d. Students will need to develop a sense of what is proper attire for the professional world.
   e. Young people are not learning to become self-sufficient with a strict uniform policy.

Wearing Uniforms In Schools

Paragraph 5

Uniforms, particularly **outfits** that **require specific style** and color **schemes**, can run a **pretty** penny, making it **difficult** for parents to have the money to spend. Parents with **young** children in elementary grades are especially **vulnerable** to rising clothing costs, because younger kids often play in their clothes at **recess** and after school and are not **careful** about **preserving** the **quality** of their clothes. Often, parents are **forced** to replace shirts, pants and sweaters, among other pieces, during the school year **multiple** times to **ensure** that their kids meet the **existing** uniform **requirements**. Further, young kids often **grow** taller during their school years forcing parents to **continuously purchase** new clothing that fits. Eliminating uniforms will enable parents to shop once for clothes and save money for their children's future.

Vocabulary Building

Exercise A: Choose the option (**a**, **b**, **c** or **d**) which fits best each sentence.

1. Designer clothes cost a .... penny.
   a. color   **c. pretty**
   b. specific   d. difficult

2. Many children at school feel .... because of bullying.
   a. vulnerable   c. multiple
   b. careful   d. existing

Exercise B: Fill in the blanks in the following sentences using words from the box. You may need to change the word. There are 2 extra words in the box you do not need to use.

a. preserve	b. ensure	c. purchase	d. force	e. require	f. grow

1. The consumers are now .....purchasing..... the new products at a discount.
2. New generations should .....preserve..... the environment and protect it in any way possible.
3. The high rates of unemployment are expected ......to force...... many people to go abroad.
4. The new rules were introduced to ......ensure....... that all students are equally treated.

Exercise C: Fill in the definitions using words from the box below. There are 2 extra words in the box that you do not need to use.

a. outfit	b. style	c. requirement	d. quality	e. scheme	f. recess

1. .....Recess........ is a break in school.
2. .....Requirement.. means the prerequisite to do something.
3. .....Scheme........ refers to a system or arrangement.
4. .....Style.......... is the way something is done.

Exercise D: Fill in the chart with the derivatives of the given adjectives or adverbs. Then, provide one **synonym** and one **antonym**, taking into account their meaning in the specific text above.

	Verb	Noun	Adjective	Adverb
1.	continue	continuity/ continuation	continuous	continuously
2.	multiply	multiplication	multiple	multiply
3.	specify	specification	specific	specifically
4.	-	youth	young	youthfully

		Synonym	Antonym
1.	continuously	constantly	intermittently
2.	multiple	various	uniform
3.	specific	particular	general
4.	young	juvenile	old

Exercise E: Write 4 sentences using the following words: **uniform**, **general**, **old**, **intermittently**. You must write 1 sentence for each of these words. Use between 8 and 15 words in each sentence. (Suggested Answers)

1. The company applied uniform policy in all its subsidiaries.
2. In general, his health is in good condition but he should avoid working too much.
3. My mum used to warn me that old habits die hard.
4. The strange object appeared intermittently in the sky.

Wearing Uniforms In Schools

Paragraph 5

A Uniforms, particularly outfits that require specific style and color schemes, can run a pretty penny, making it difficult for parents to have the money to spend. Parents with young children in elementary grades are especially **vulnerable** to rising clothing costs, because younger kids often play in their clothes at recess and after school and are not careful about preserving the quality of their clothes. **B** Often, parents are forced to replace shirts, pants and sweaters, among other pieces, during the school year multiple times to ensure that their kids meet the existing uniform requirements. <u>Further, young kids often grow taller during their school years forcing parents to continuously purchase new clothing that fits</u>. **C** Eliminating uniforms will enable parents to shop once for clothes and save money for their children's future. **D**

Reading Comprehension

1. The word **vulnerable** in §5 is closest in meaning to
   a. enriched.
   b. unprotected.
   c. ridiculed.
   d. unorganized.

2. Based on the text, what type of financial impact do uniforms have on parents?
   a. They bring clothing costs down across the board.
   b. They have little effect on the clothing costs for parents.
   c. They increase yearly clothing costs particularly if the students are quite young.
   d. They eliminate the need to buy new clothes for generations of students.

3. Why does the author refer to the costs of clothes for parents particularly with young children?
   a. to show that it's easy for these parents to acquire new clothes
   b. to illustrate the importance of making school uniforms a requirement at schools
   c. to make the case that it's cheaper for parents in this situation to fund uniform costs
   d. to advance the idea that uniform costs hurt their ability to save more money

4. Which sentence below best expresses the essential information in the underlined sentence in §5?
   a. As children grow, they need new clothes, forcing parents to spend more money.
   b. As children grow, they grow into their clothes, whereby parents spend less cash.
   c. As children grow, their uniforms fit better so that parents don't need to pay for adjustments.
   d. As children grow, their desire for clothes diminishes, enabling parents to save money.

5. Based on the passage, which of the following is **NOT** an item parents need to replace as their kids grow?
   a. trousers
   b. jewelry
   c. shirts
   d. coats

6. Look at the four squares, **A**, **B**, **C** and **D**, which indicate where the following sentence could be added to the passage. Where would the sentence best fit? Right Answer: C

   Thus, we need to make it easier and not harder for parents to fund their children's education.

7. An introductory sentence for a brief summary of the passage is provided below. Complete the summary by selecting the **THREE** answer choices that express the most important ideas in the passage. Some sentences do not belong in the summary because they express ideas that are not presented in the passage or are ideas of minor importance. **This question is worth 2 points.**

   Eliminating a school uniform policy will help parents to save money to help fund other parts of their children's lives.

   a. School uniforms are costly especially when parents have young children that are still growing.
   b. Parents need to buy new clothes throughout the school year to meet the uniform policy.
   c. Children are always responsible with their clothes and never damage them during recess.
   d. With the money saved on uniforms, parents have more money to dedicate for college education.
   e. School uniform policies help parents to control their yearly living costs.

Wearing Uniforms In Schools

Paragraph 6

Finally, one of the most **important attributes** school uniforms **hurt** is a student's **creativity**. Young people like me, namely those who are growing from **childhood** to becoming young adults, are **abounding** with creativity and **insight**, desiring greatly to **express** ourselves in all that we choose to **undertake**. By making us wear school uniforms every day, schools **retard** our creative **impulses** and **instincts** based on **guidelines** that are rather **arbitrary**. **Permitting** students to wear what they choose is the **first** step in letting us realize our **full potential** as **innovative** human beings. Don't force us to **conform** and become **mere** robots when we can make great **contributions** to humanity. Let us wear what makes us feel **comfortable** and you will see our confidence and personal **identity** grow.

Vocabulary Building

Exercise A: Choose the option (**a**, **b**, **c** or **d**) which fits best each sentence.

1. Creativity is an important .... which is very much sought after.

    a. guideline   **c. attribute**

    b. identity   **d.** potential

2. She felt like her teacher helped her to develop her .... potential.

    a. comfortable   **c.** mere

    b. first   **d. full**

Exercise B: Fill in the blanks in the following sentences using words from the box below. There are 2 extra words in the box you do not need to use. You may change the words.

a. express	**b.** abound	**c.** conform	**d.** undertake	**e.** permit	**f.** retard

1. Younger generations ....*abound*.......... with innovative ideas and creativity.
2. The municipality ..*will undertake*.. the task of rebuilding the school soon.
3. Financial problems are expected ......*to retard*...... development in the private sector.
4. The head teacher promised parents that he *will/would not* ...... any violation of the rules. *permit*

Exercise C: Fill in the definitions using words from the box below. There are 2 extra words in the box that you do not need to use.

a. creativity	**b.** impulse	**c.** instinct	**d.** contribution	**e.** childhood	**f.** insight

1. ......*Instinct*........ means a natural power that gives one intuition.
2. ......*Creativity*..... refers to inventing new things.
3. ......*Impulse*...... is the urge one feels to act without reason.
4. ...*Contribution*.... is one's share of aiding in something.

Exercise D: Fill in the chart with the derivatives of the given adjectives or adverbs. Then, provide one **synonym** and one **antonym**, taking into account their meaning in the specific text above.

	Verb	Noun	Adjective	Adverb
1.	finalize	finalization/finality	final	finally
2.	–	arbitrariness	arbitrary	arbitrarily
3.	innovate	innovation	innovative	innovatively
4.	–	importance	important	importantly

		Synonym	Antonym
1.	finally	overall	firstly
2.	arbitrary	random/inconsistent	reasoned/consistent
3.	innovative	original	old-fashioned
4.	important	essential	unimportant

Exercise E: Write 4 sentences using the following words: consistent, old-fashioned, unimportant, firstly. You must write 1 sentence for each of these words. Use between 8 and 15 words in each sentence.

(Suggested Answers)

1. His work has been consistent throughout all these years.
2. It is about time we stopped dealing with issues in an old-fashioned way.
3. Please do not waste my time with unimportant matters.
4. Firstly, it is worth mentioning that there is no intention to change the rules.

Wearing Uniforms In Schools

Paragraph 6

A Finally, one of the most important attributes school uniforms hurt is a student's creativity. Young people like me, namely those who are growing from childhood to becoming young adults, are abounding with creativity and insight, desiring greatly to express ourselves in all that we choose to **undertake**. By making us wear school uniforms every day, schools retard our creative impulses and instincts based on guidelines that are rather arbitrary. **B** Permitting students to wear what they choose is the first step in letting us realize our full potential as innovative human beings. Don't force us to conform and become mere robots when we can make great contributions to humanity. **C** Let us wear what makes us feel comfortable and you'll see our confidence and personal identity grow. **D**

Reading Comprehension

1. The word **undertake** in §6 is closest in meaning to
   - **a.** endeavor.
   - **b.** fight.
   - **c.** classify.
   - **d.** require.

2. Based on the text, in what are school uniform policies hurting students?
   - **a.** personal responsibility
   - **b.** originality
   - **c.** comfort
   - **d.** conformity

3. What is the consequence, according to the author, of forcing students to conform to a uniform policy?
   - **a.** Students become responsible office workers.
   - **b.** Students are not prepared to navigate an organized corporate culture.
   - **c.** Students aren't able to contribute their creative viewpoint to society.
   - **d.** Students develop a lack of respect for authority and their peers in society.

4. Which sentence below best expresses the essential information in the underlined sentence in §6?
   - **a.** School uniform policies are hurting the innovative tendencies of students based on random rules.
   - **b.** School uniform policies encourage students to think outside the box based on a set of fixed guidelines.
   - **c.** School uniform policies limit the ability of a student to fail regardless of the thinking behind the rules.
   - **d.** School uniform policies are making it easier for students to learn in schools despite the resistance of parents.

5. Based on the passage, which of the following is **NOT** a characteristic students naturally have?
   - **a.** imagination
   - **b.** originality
   - **c.** intuition
   - **d.** cynicism

6. Look at the four squares, **A**, **B**, **C** and **D**, which indicate where the following sentence could be added to the passage. Where would the sentence best fit? Right Answer: B

   In other words, the reasoning for why we have to wear uniforms doesn't seem that convincing.

7. An introductory sentence for a brief summary of the passage is provided below. Complete the summary by selecting the **THREE** answer choices that express the most important ideas in the passage. Some sentences do not belong in the summary because they express ideas that are not presented in the passage or are ideas of minor importance. **This question is worth 2 points.**

   The idea of school uniforms cuts against the ideals and values schools claim to seek to develop.

   - **a.** Mandatory school uniforms encourage students to think in unconventional ways.
   - **b.** Not having to wear school uniforms would help students express their originality.
   - **c.** Schools should let students dress as they please to further establish their own individual identities.
   - **d.** Teachers should treat their students the same, making them dress, learn and behave the same.
   - **e.** If schools want students to be innovative, then they should trust them to dress themselves uniquely.

Debate 4

Wearing Uniforms In Schools: The Advantages

Paragraph 1

When I was my daughter's age, a shirt, tie and blazer were not my **ideal wardrobe** choices, but, given the recent debate on school uniforms, I wouldn't give up on the idea of making them the rule. A school uniform, from my **viewpoint**, is like wearing a **badge** of honor as it creates a sense of school identity and is an important **part** of growing up as a young person. One of my son's friends agrees and recently told me "Uniforms show that you are part of a team, an important **organization.** Wearing one expresses the **idea** that we're all in this together." I agree and think that by wearing one you're saying "Respect me" because "I'm buying into what the organization is all about." Of course, my kids hate me for thinking this way.

Paragraph 2

My children's **consternation** aside, one of my son's teachers furthered this idea in terms of **pride** and focus. She believes they give students a strong sense of belonging and **forge** a sense of identity in the community. Beginning this school year, my kids have to wear a shirt, blazer and tie with pressed khakis every day. Before, they only had to wear a polo shirt with khakis. Of course, many students and parents have fought the change. Others, though, like the idea, **arguing** that the polo was a bit **childish**. I think uniforms help students to **focus** more in school and teach them how to dress **professionally** when they enter the working world. I **concur** with those experts who contend they reduce distraction, thereby making students more focused on their courses.

Paragraph 3

Moreover, uniforms take away some of the problems of peer pressure in school. Forms of peer pressure, of course, will continue with or without uniforms; however, when everyone is dressed the same, concerns about what you look like are reduced significantly. There's no envy or feeling of need to be dressed in the latest trends, which only increases an already **substantial** financial burden placed on parents. Bullies have one less **piece** of potential **ammunition** to bother someone. I read a study recently that found 160,000 children, who attended institutions that did not **require** a uniform, missed school daily because of fear of being bullied or threats of **intimidation**. Though attire may not be the exact reason for the bullying, the uniform can **serve** as a **solace** for some students who might otherwise be attacked.

Paragraph 4

As I mentioned a bit earlier, school uniforms are also a great way for parents to save money. Education isn't getting any cheaper, especially at the university level, so finding ways to save money early on are in the best interest for students and parents **alike**. Uniforms are less costly than having to buy a wardrobe of **seasonal outfits** every year. Most schools have **recommended suppliers** and uniform **outlets** that offer great **value** to parents. These relationships are **useful** and help parents to control their **costs**. When schools decide to **alter** their uniform with, for instance, a new **logo**, material, or color, the changes are traditionally limited to one or two pieces helping to keep costs affordable. This, ultimately, further keeps the **focus** of schools on education rather than outside distractions like fashion and apparel.

Paragraph 5

I get it that kids want to have fun and be cool. I was no different. When I was my children's age, I wanted to dress like James Dean and Marlon Brando. The idea of wearing a uniform would have bummed me out. But, as a parent, I'm not trying to be cool. I want my kids to **excel** in life and thus, I believe, school uniforms are the best thing for students, parents and schools alike. It makes it easier for kids to get ready for school in the morning and prepares them for life, when how they dress for work will be more streamlined. Students don't fall as easy to peer pressure and look focused and serious in their attire. I know I wouldn't want to wear one on my own time, but it gives students a sense of community and belonging to something bigger than themselves. School uniforms aren't necessarily chic, yet that's **precisely** why I think they should be required.

Vocabulary Building

Exercise A: Choose the option (**a**, **b**, **c** or **d**) which fits best each sentence.

1. It is not ……. your best interest to share your thoughts with James.
   - **a. in**
   - **b.** on
   - **c.** at
   - **d.** of

2. The new course offered great ……. to the student's education.
   - **a.** piece
   - **b.** badge
   - **c.** logo
   - **d. value**

3. In schools, boys and girls should be treated ……….. .
   - **a.** like
   - **b. alike**
   - **c.** precisely
   - **d.** professionally

4. To keep the ……. of maintenance affordable, we have to make some cuts.
   - **a.** supplier
   - **b.** viewpoint
   - **c.** focus
   - **d. cost**

5. She felt ……. out when her boyfriend laughed at her.
   - **a.** ideal
   - **b.** substantial
   - **c. bummed**
   - **d.** childish

6. He tried to resist ………. pressure and be himself.
   - **a. peer**
   - **b.** idea
   - **c.** part
   - **d.** wardrobe

Exercise B: Fill in the blanks in the following sentences using words from the box. You may need to change the word. There are 2 extra words in the box you do not need to use.

a. alter	**b.** recommend	**c.** concur	**d.** forge	**e.** excel	**f.** argue	**g.** require	**h.** serve

1. The coach managed …… to forge …… a sense of solidarity to the team.
2. I strongly …… recommend … that you wear less casual clothes at the office.
3. The skills she developed at school helped her …… excel ……… at work.
4. Hopefully, parents and teachers …… will concur …. on the need to adjust class schedule.
5. The position …… does not require … IT skills. You can be trained later.
6. They will need to ……… alter ……… their bad habits if they want to be accepted.

Exercise C: Fill in the definitions using words from the box below. There are 2 extra words in the box that you do not need to use.

a. organization	**b.** consternation	**c.** pride	**d.** intimidation	**e.** solace	**f.** ammunition	**g.** outfit	**h.** outlet

1. …… Consternation …… is a feeling of confusion.
2. …… Ammunition …… means the material used for guns during battle.
3. …… Intimidation …… refers to the act of scaring someone.
4. …… Outfit …… is what one wears.
5. …… Pride …… means the feeling of self-respect.
6. …… Solace …… is a feeling of comfort.

Exercise D: Fill in the chart with the derivatives of the given adjectives or adverbs. Then, provide one **synonym** and one **antonym**, taking into account their meaning in the specific text above.

	Verb	Noun	Adjective	Adverb
1.	idealize	idea	ideal	ideally
2.	profess(ionalize)	profession	professional	professionally
3.	-	child(hood)	childish	childishly
4.	substantiate	substance	substantial	substantially
5.	season	season	seasonal	seasonally
6.	use	use/usefulness	useful	usefully

		Synonym	Antonym
1.	ideal	perfect	problematic
2.	professionally	flawlessly	unprofessionally
3.	childish	immature	mature
4.	substantial	significant	insignificant
5.	seasonal	temporal	permanent
6.	useful	practical	useless

Exercise E: Write 6 sentences using the following words: problematic, mature, permanent, useless, unprofessionally, insignificant. You must write 1 sentence for each of these words. Use between 8 and 15 words in each sentence.

(Suggested Answers)

1. Dealing with eccentric students was more problematic than expected.
2. Mature students can learn faster and are more cooperative in class.
3. This is a permanent situation that is difficult to handle.
4. The new discipline measure was completely useless when it came to bullying.
5. The job was so unprofessionally done that the customer asked for a refund.
6. His contribution to the reform was insignificant.

Debate 4

TOEFL Exam Practice: Reading Comprehension

Debate 4

Paragraph 1

When I was my daughter's age, a shirt, tie and blazer were not my **ideal** wardrobe choices, but, given the recent debate on school uniforms, I wouldn't give up on the idea of making them the rule. A school uniform, from my viewpoint, is like wearing a badge of honor as it creates a sense of school identity and is an important part of growing up as a young person. One of my son's friends agrees and recently told me "Uniforms show that you are part of a team, an important organization. Wearing one expresses the idea that we're all in this together." I agree and think that by wearing one you're saying "Respect me" because "I'm buying into what the organization is all about." Of course, my kids hate me for thinking this way.

1. The word **ideal** in §1 is closest in meaning to
   a. opposite.
   b. first.
   c. worst.
   d. overrated.

2. According to the text, why does one of the friends of the author's child like the idea of school uniforms?
   a. They make him feel estranged from his peers.
   b. They make him feel as though the other children are superior to him.
   c. They make him feel as though he is a part of an institution.
   d. They make him feel as though too much emphasis is put on uniforms.

Paragraph 2

My children's consternation aside, one of my son's teachers furthered this idea in terms of pride and focus. She believes they give students a strong sense of belonging and **forge** a sense of identity in the community. Beginning this school year, my kids have to wear a shirt, blazer and tie with pressed khakis every day. Before, they only had to wear a polo shirt with khakis. Of course, many students and parents have fought the change. Others, though, like the idea, arguing that the polo was a bit **childish**. I think uniforms help students to focus more in school and teach them how to dress professionally when they enter the working world. I concur with those experts who contend they reduce distraction, thereby making students more focused on their courses.

3. The phrase **forge** in §2 is closest in meaning to
   a. develop.   c. unmask.
   b. hurt.   d. frequent.

4. The word **childish** in §2 is closest in meaning to
   a. elderly.   c. immature.
   b. neutral.   d. flamboyant.

5. What is the author's reasoning for wearing uniforms in this paragraph?
   a. Uniforms make students seem like adults.
   b. Uniforms increase recreational time in schools.
   c. Uniforms really don't matter in terms of how children focus.
   d. Uniforms help students to concentrate better on learning.

Paragraph 3

Moreover, uniforms take away some of the problems of peer pressure in school. Forms of peer pressure, of course, will continue with or without uniforms; however, when everyone is dressed the same, concerns about what you look like are reduced significantly. There's no envy or feeling of need to be dressed in the latest trends, which only increases an already **substantial** financial burden placed on parents. Bullies have one less piece of potential ammunition to bother someone. I read a study recently that found 160,000 children, who attended institutions that did not require a uniform, missed school daily because of fear of being bullied or threats of **intimidation**. Though attire may not be the exact reason for the bullying, the uniform can serve as a solace for some students who might otherwise be attacked.

6. According to the passage, what is the relationship between school uniforms and school attendance?
   a. Students who wear uniforms are bullied more and don't go to school.
   b. Students who wear uniforms attend school more regularly.
   c. Students who wear uniforms are bullied more but still come to school regularly.
   d. Students who wear uniforms choose not to come to school as often.

7. The word **substantial** in §3 is closest in meaning to
   a. unimportant.   c. weak.
   b. realistic.   d. significant.

8. The word **intimidation** in §3 is closest in meaning to
   a. compassion.   c. bullying.
   b. respect.   d. intervention.

Paragraph 4

As I mentioned a bit earlier, school uniforms are also a great way for parents to save money. Education isn't getting any cheaper, especially at the university level, so finding ways to save money early on are in the best interest for students and parents alike. Uniforms are less costly than having to buy a wardrobe of **seasonal** outfits every year. Most schools have recommended suppliers and uniform outlets that offer great value to parents. These relationships are useful and help parents to control their costs. When schools decide to alter their uniform with, for instance, a new logo, material, or color, the changes are traditionally limited to one or two pieces helping to keep costs affordable. This, ultimately, further keeps the focus of schools on education rather than outside distractions like fashion and apparel.

9. Based on the passage, the financial significance of uniforms is
    a. that they force parents to spend more money on clothes.
    b. that they enable parents to receive less value for their money.
    c. that they help parents save for the future education of their children.
    d. that they compel parents to ask for discounts from school uniform suppliers.

10. The word **seasonal** in §4 is closest in meaning to
    a. consistent.
    b. fixed.
    c. temporal.
    d. restricted.

11. According to the text, one can infer that the cost of education is
    a. falling even though the cost of uniforms is rising.
    b. rising overall regardless of the price of uniforms.
    c. remaining the same as the price of uniforms increase.
    d. becoming insignificant with the seasonal approach to uniforms.

Paragraph 5

I get it that kids want to have fun and be cool. I was no different. When I was my children's age, I wanted to dress like James Dean and Marlon Brando. The idea of wearing a uniform would have **bummed me out**. But, as a parent, I'm not trying to be cool. I want my kids to excel in life and thus, I believe, school uniforms are the best thing for students, parents and schools alike. It makes it easier for kids to get ready for school in the morning and prepares them for life, when how they dress for work will be more streamlined. Students don't fall as easy to peer pressure and look focused and serious in their attire. I know I wouldn't want to wear one on my own time, but it gives students a sense of community and belonging to something bigger than themselves. School uniforms aren't necessarily chic, yet that's precisely why I think they should be required.

12. The phrase **bummed me out** in §5 is closest in meaning to
    a. made happy.
    b. caused confusion.
    c. caused unhappiness.
    d. made irate.

13. According to the passage, one of the life lessons of school uniforms is that
    a. students develop dress habits for the professional world.
    b. students learn how to dress for sporting events.
    c. students develop the ability to color coordinate apparel items and accessories.
    d. students learn to be individuals and express their creativity.

Paragraphs 1 to 5

14. An introductory sentence for a brief summary of the passage is provided below. Complete the summary by selecting the **THREE** answer choices that express the most important ideas in the passage. Some sentences do not belong in the summary because they express ideas that are not presented in the passage or are ideas of minor importance. **This question is worth 2 points.**

    School uniforms are a great way to instill pride in students and prepare them for the professional world.

    a. Students develop a sense of identity within the context of a larger organization.
    b. Students learn to become unique individuals able to make their own choices about how they dress.
    c. Distractions in education are reduced when students have to wear a fixed outfit to school.
    d. Bullies have more opportunities to intimidate their peers when everyone must wear the same thing.
    e. Parents are able to save money having more resources to fund higher education.

15. Select the appropriate sentences from the answer choices and match them to the characterization of uniforms. **TWO** of the answer choices will **NOT** be used. **This question is worth 3 points.**

    a. Students become invested in being part of a large organization.
    b. Children don't develop the same personal judgment skills when wearing a uniform.
    c. Teachers spend more time punishing bullies when kids wear uniforms.
    d. Students are more focused on their studies and more respectful of each other.
    e. School bullying decreases and student attendance improves with school uniforms.
    f. With school uniforms children don't develop an individual identity as much.
    g. Parents spend more money on yearly clothing costs.

Benefits of School Uniforms:	A/D/E
Drawbacks of School Uniforms:	B/F

Debate 4

Experiments on animals

Paragraph 1

While few would **dispute** the incredible **advances** made in the field of medical **research** over recent years, the method of research **employed** to **yield** such results is a **source** of **controversy**. **Funding** for medical research as well as product safety testing is **channeled** primarily into vivisection or the **experimentation** on live animals under **laboratory** conditions. **Alternative** methods of research are **sidelined** in the **perpetual quest** to find cures for disease or to ensure that a product is safe for humans to use. The result is that cures are found and products are proved safe for **domestic** use. But at what cost to the animals themselves, often forced to **undergo** experiments that are **tantamount** to **torture**? And can such experiments ever really be justified on any level or are they a **hangover** from a **bygone** era of science that is now **hopelessly anachronistic**?

Vocabulary Building

Exercise A: Choose the option (**a**, **b**, **c** or **d**) which fits best each sentence.

1. I'm afraid the system you've been working with is now greatly ………. .

   a. tantamount   **c.** domestic

   b. alternative   **d. anachronistic**

2. My fear of spiders is definitely a ………. from my childhood.

   a. source   **c. hangover**

   b. torture   **d.** bygone

Exercise B: Fill in the blanks in the following sentences using words from the box below. There are 2 extra words in the box you do not need to use. You cannot change the words.

a. dispute	**b.** employ	**c.** channel	**d.** undergo	**e.** sideline	**f.** yield

1. It was wrong of her friends to ……dispute…… her intensions.
2. He will ……employ…… all means to achieve his goal.
3. Unfortunately the building must ……undergo…… renovations.
4. New methods are certain to ……yield…… promising results in the future.

Exercise C: Fill in the definitions using words from the box below. There are 2 extra words in the box that you do not need to use.

a. advance	**b.** research	**c.** funding	**d.** controversy	**e.** quest	**f.** laboratory

1. ……Controversy…… means dispute, especially a public one, between sides holding opposing views.
2. ……Quest…… is the act of looking for or seeking something.
3. ……Advance…… is an improvement; a progress in development.
4. ……Funding…… refers to the financial resources provided to make a project possible.

Exercise D: Fill in the chart with the derivatives of the given adjectives or adverbs. Then, provide one **synonym** and one **antonym**, taking into account their meaning in the specific text above.

	Verb	**Noun**	**Adjective**	**Adverb**
1.	alter	alternative	alternative	alternatively
2.	hope	hope	hopeless	hopelessly
3.	justify	justification	justified	justifiably
4.	perpetuate	perpetuity	perpetual	perpetually

		Synonym	**Antonym**
1.	alternative	different/variant	conventional
2.	hopelessly	desperately/sadly	hopefully/confidently
3.	justified	reasonable/understandable	unjustified/unacceptable
4.	perpetual	endless/continuous	brief/finite

Exercise E: Write 4 sentences using the following words: unjustified, conventional, hopefully, brief. You must write 1 sentence for each of these words. Use between 8 and 15 words in each sentence.   (Suggested Answers)

1. Everyone agreed that the police action was completely unjustified.
2. Calling a man 'mister' is a conventional form of address.
3. Hopefully there will be an agreement between the two sides soon.
4. He gave a brief account of the incident to the police.

Experiments on animals

Paragraph 1

While few would dispute the incredible advances made in the field of medical research over recent years, the method of research employed to yield such results is a source of controversy. **A** Funding for medical research as well as product safety testing is channeled primarily into vivisection or the experimentation on live animals under laboratory conditions. Alternative methods of research are **sidelined** in the perpetual quest to find cures for disease or to ensure that a product is safe for humans to use. **B** The result is that cures are found and products are proved safe for domestic use. **C** But at what cost, though, to the animals themselves, often forced to undergo experiments that are tantamount to torture? **D** And can such experiments ever really be justified on any level or are they a hangover from a bygone era of science that is now hopelessly anachronistic?

Reading Comprehension

1. The word **sidelined** in §1 is closest in meaning to
   a. relegated.   c. denounced.
   b. ignored.   d. ridiculed.

2. According to the passage, why is medical research a questionable practice?
   a. It requires too much funding.
   b. The studies are flawed.
   c. No credible results are forthcoming from such research.
   d. Research involves experimentation on live animals.

3. What is the main objection of the author to vivisection?
   a. Too much research is spent on developing products safe for domestic use.
   b. It is costly to keep animals for laboratory research.
   c. Scant regard is paid to the animals' living conditions.
   d. The practice involves extreme discomfort to the animals concerned.

4. Which sentence below best expresses the essential information in the underlined sentence in §1?
   a. Drawing upon historical scientific practice is a questionable exercise.
   b. Demonstrable results can be obtained when using past scientific methodology.
   c. The field of scientific research is developing rapidly.
   d. The golden era of science is long gone.

5. All of the following are true of animal research **EXCEPT**
   a. funding for vivisection is prioritized in medical research.
   b. animal research generates little interest.
   c. vivisection may have little relevance in the modern medical world.
   d. it is a constant challenge to find domestic and medical products that are safe to use.

6. Look at the four squares, **A**, **B**, **C** and **D**, which indicate where the following sentence could be added to the passage. Where would the sentence best fit?   Right Answer: A

   This is mainly due to the questionable practice of animal experimentation.

7. An introductory sentence for a brief summary of the passage is provided below. Complete the summary by selecting the **THREE** answer choices that express the most important ideas in the passage. Some sentences do not belong in the summary because they express ideas that are not presented in the passage or are ideas of minor importance. **This question is worth 2 points.**

   Medical research has come on in leaps and bounds but in the process has incited heated debate.

   a. Financial support for animal research is considered paramount.
   b. Money is diverted into unworthy forms of research.
   c. There is a failure to explore other forms of research.
   d. Many products have failed to be given the all-clear in research experiments.
   e. Vivisection is barbaric, cruel and a remnant from past scientific methods of research.
   f. In hindsight, vivisection will probably be vindicated as a method of research.

Debate 5

Experiments on animals

Paragraph 2

We are all **brainwashed** into thinking that all we need is to find a **cure** for a **disease**; whether it be for a **commonplace** illness, like Rubella, or more **serious** illnesses, such as AIDS or cancer, in order to **improve** the **quality** of our lives. Of course, finding a cure for these diseases would be a **game changer** but have we ever **really paused** to **contemplate**? What if we could **prevent** these diseases **entirely** so we didn't have to find a cure for them in the first place? The **aphorism** 'Prevention is better than cure,' has a lot to be said for it. Time and **effort** spent in curing a disease far **exceeds** the time and effort **deployed** to prevent disease. This is surely a travesty of science.

Vocabulary Building

Exercise A: Choose the option (**a**, **b**, **c** or **d**) which fits best each sentence.

1. The company's new launch is definitely going to be a(n) ....
   a. quality
   b. prevention
   c. game changer
   d. aphorism

2. Despite the risks, cosmetic surgery is now ....
   a. commonplace
   b. deployed
   c. brainwashed
   d. entire

Exercise B: Fill in the blanks in the following sentences using words from the box below. There are 2 extra words in the box you do not need to use. You cannot change the words.

a. cure	**b.** quality	**c.** aphorism	**d.** effort	**e.** disease

1. Unfortunately there has been no ......cure........ found yet for your condition.
2. I have concluded that this .....aphorism..... accounts for all human behavior.
3. The ......disease...... spread to large parts of the country.

Exercise C: Fill in the definitions using words from the box below. There are 2 extra words in the box that you do not need to use.

a. improve	**b.** pause	**c.** exceed	**d.** contemplate	**e.** prevent

1. To ......improve...... means to raise to a more desirable condition.
2. To ......prevent...... is to impede; keep something from happening.
3. To ......exceed...... means to be greater in quantity than something else.

Exercise D: Fill in the chart with the derivatives of the given adjectives or adverbs. Then, provide one **synonym** and one **antonym**, taking into account their meaning in the specific text above.

	Verb	Noun	Adjective	Adverb			Synonym	Antonym
1.	brainwash	brainwashing	brainwashed	-	**1.**	brainwashed	influenced/persuaded	unconvinced
2.	realize	reality/realization	real	really	**2.**	really	actually/truly	professedly/supposedly
3.	-	seriousness	serious	seriously	**3.**	serious	critical/severe/threatening	minor/commonplace
4.	-	entirety/entireness	entire	entirely	**4.**	entirely	totally/altogether	partly/partially

Exercise E: Write 4 sentences using the following words: partly, unconvinced, supposedly, minor. You must write 1 sentence for each of these words. Use between 8 and 15 words in each sentence. (Suggested Answers)

1. His account of what happened was only partly accurate.
2. I'm afraid that I remain unconvinced about his innocence.
3. He was supposedly one of the most talented leaders in world history.
4. We do not intend to spend any more time on such a minor issue.

Experiments on animals

Paragraph 2

We are all brainwashed into thinking that all we need is to find a cure for a disease; whether it be for a commonplace illness, like Rubella, or more serious illnesses, such as AIDS or cancer, to improve the quality of our lives. **A** Of course, finding a cure for these diseases would be a **game changer** but have we ever really paused to contemplate? What if we could prevent these diseases entirely so we didn't have to find a cure for them in the first place? The aphorism 'Prevention is better than cure,' has a lot to be said for it. **B** Time and effort spent in curing a disease far exceeds the time and effort deployed to prevent disease. **C** This is surely a travesty of science. **D**

Reading Comprehension

1. The word **game changer** in §2 is closest in meaning to
   a. conquest.
   b. benefit.
   c. revolution.
   d. challenge.

2. Based on the passage, our belief that the eradication of illness would enhance our lives is a belief that is
   a. misguided.
   b. unfounded.
   c. valid.
   d. reprehensible.

3. The current attitude to disease needs to be
   a. researched.
   b. readdressed.
   c. perpetuated.
   d. derided.

4. Which sentence below best expresses the essential information in the underlined sentence in §2?
   a. Many people have a lot to say on the subject of 'Prevention is better than cure.'
   b. The saying 'Prevention is better than cure,' is multi-layered in meaning.
   c. There is more than an element of truth in the old adage 'Prevention is better than cure.'
   d. Although the concept of 'Prevention is better than cure,' is a sound one, not many put the words into practice.

5. Focusing primarily on curing illness is hoped to facilitate all of the following **EXCEPT**
   a. disease prevention.
   b. a better life.
   c. a cure for life-threatening illnesses.
   d. remedies for everyday illnesses.

6. Look at the four squares, **A**, **B**, **C** and **D**, which indicate where the following sentence could be added to the passage. Where would the sentence best fit?

   Right Answer: B

   Such a concept is not radical, just practical.

7. An introductory sentence for a brief summary of the passage is provided below. Complete the summary by selecting the **THREE** answer choices that express the most important ideas in the passage. Some sentences do not belong in the summary because they express ideas that are not presented in the passage or are ideas of minor importance. **This question is worth 2 points.**

   A widespread belief is that finding a cure for illnesses will enhance our lives.

   a. It is widely held that a panacea for all diseases does exist.
   b. If a panacea were to be found, it would be revolutionary.
   c. Few believe that diseases can be adequately eradicated.
   d. Curing an illness is more problematic than preventing one.
   e. Financial and physical resources expended in curing illness would be better spent on disease prevention.
   f. Scientists mislead themselves into believing they should spend money on curing, not preventing illness.

Debate 5

Experiments on animals

> **Paragraph 3**
> While **preventative measures** against a certain illness, like cancer, can **comprise** diet and exercise and **involve relatively** little time and money, cures for serious illnesses involve extremely **costly** and time-consuming therapeutic **procedures**. These **include** chemotherapy and **radiation** as well as the taking of expensive drugs to **suppress tumor** growth. **Side-effects** of these procedures and **drugs** apart, it is obviously **vastly preferable** to prevent such illnesses from the **outset** than **set about** trying to find a cure when the illness **has taken a hold on** the **patient**'s body. Therefore, it is a sad irony that **governments** channel tens of millions of dollars **annually** into vivisection, but **considerably** fewer dollars each year into funding alternative medical research. And things don't look set to change anywhere in the near future, either.

Vocabulary Building

Exercise A: Choose the option (**a**, **b**, **c** or **d**) which fits best each sentence.

1. The number of surgical ………. performed in the hospital went down.
   - **a.** side-effects
   - **c.** measures
   - **b.** procedures
   - **d.** drugs

2. The jury was greatly confused as they heard two ………. different accounts of what happened.
   - **a.** relatively
   - **c.** costly
   - **b.** vastly
   - **d.** annually

Exercise B: Fill in the blanks in the following sentences using the correct form of the words from the box below. There are 2 extra words in the box you do not need to use.

a. comprise	**b.** involve	**c.** include	**d.** suppress	**e.** set about	**f.** take a hold on

1. The emperor …… suppressed …… any attempt of a rebellion before the 1820s.
2. Recently, they …… have set about …… solving a problem that has been troubling them for years.
3. The union is …… comprised …… of 50 States.
4. Both men were …… involved …… in the crime.

Exercise C: Fill in the definitions using words from the box below. There are 2 extra words in the box that you do not need to use.

a. government	**b.** radiation	**c.** tumor	**d.** side-effect	**e.** outset	**f.** patient

1. …… Government …… means the executive policy-making body of a political community.
2. …… Patient …… is one who receives medical care and treatment.
3. …… Tumor …… is defined as a mass of tissue formed by a new growth of cells.
4. …… Radiation …… means emission of energy in the form of rays or waves.

Exercise D: Fill in the chart with the derivatives of the given adjectives or adverbs. Then, provide one **synonym** and one **antonym**, taking into account their meaning in the specific text above.

	Verb	Noun	Adjective	Adverb
1.	prevent	prevention	preventative	preventatively
2.	relate	relation/relative	relative	relatively
3.	consider	consideration	considerable	considerably
4.	prefer	preference	preferable	preferably

		Synonym	Antonym
1.	preventative	precautionary	facilitating/forwarding
2.	relatively	quite/somewhat	extremely
3.	considerably	significantly/greatly	slightly
4.	preferable	desirable/favored	undesirable

Exercise E: Write 4 sentences using the following words: slightly, facilitating, extremely, undesirable. You must write 1 sentence for each of these words. Use between 8 and 15 words in each sentence. (Suggested Answers)

1. This case is slightly different than the ones treated before.
2. Revising regularly the material is guaranteed to have a facilitating effect on your memory.
3. I think it is extremely important to bear in mind the instructions given.
4. We cannot assure you that there will not be any undesirable effects by the treatment.

Debate 5

Experiments on animals

Paragraph 3

While preventive measures against a certain illness, like cancer, can **comprise** diet and exercise and involve relatively little time and money, cures for serious illnesses involve extremely costly and time-consuming therapeutic procedures. These include chemotherapy and radiation as well as surgery and the taking of expensive drugs to suppress tumor growth. **A** Side-effects of these procedures and drugs apart, it is obviously vastly preferable to prevent such illnesses from the outset than set about trying to find a cure when the illness has taken a hold on the patient's body. **B** Therefore, it is a sad irony that governments channel tens of millions of dollars annually into vivisection, but considerably fewer dollars each year into funding alternative medical research. **C** And things don't look set to change anywhere in the near future, either. **D**

Reading Comprehension

1. The word **comprise** in §3 is closest in meaning to
   a. involve.
   b. advise.
   c. encourage.
   d. instigate.

2. According to the passage, what is true about life-threatening illnesses, like cancer?
   a. Treatment is prolonged and expensive.
   b. Positive outcomes are usually guaranteed.
   c. Little can be done to prevent such illnesses.
   d. A cure for such illnesses is proving elusive.

3. Why does the author refer to governments?
   a. as an example of misplaced funding into medical research
   b. to indicate the degree of involvement of this authority in medical research
   c. to show how funds into medical research are being allocated
   d. to illustrate a lack of concern by this authority over animal research

4. Which sentence below best expresses the essential information in the underlined sentence in §3?
   a. Taking precautionary measures to ward off illness rarely proves fruitful.
   b. Curing an illness is a more costly and lengthy process than preventing it in the first place.
   c. Preventive medicine needs to be complemented by medical procedures such as chemotherapy.
   d. It is wiser to invest in more costly medical procedures that cure illness than trust preventive medicine.

5. All of the following are true of preventive medicine **EXCEPT**
   a. it usually involves less expenditure than most curative measures.
   b. it was a precursor to more conventional medical practices.
   c. it can take many forms.
   d. it involves non-surgical intervention.

6. Look at the four squares, **A**, **B**, **C** and **D**, which indicate where the following sentence could be added to the passage. Where would the sentence best fit?   Right Answer: B

   It is like shutting the door after the horse has bolted.

7. An introductory sentence for a brief summary of the passage is provided below. Complete the summary by selecting the **THREE** answer choices that express the most important ideas in the passage. Some sentences do not belong in the summary because they express ideas that are not presented in the passage or are ideas of minor importance. **This question is worth 2 points.**

   Preventive medicine is vastly preferable to curative medicine, with regard to cost and time involved in curative, as compared to preventive medicine.

   a. Surgical intervention is only partially successful.
   b. It is comparatively easier to prevent rather than cure an illness.
   c. Common to both preventive and curative medicine are unforeseen side-effects.
   d. The importance of preventive medicine is universally acknowledged.
   e. Insufficient funding is given to preventive medicine.
   f. It is unlikely that there will be a sea change with regard to the apportioning of medical funding in the foreseeable future.

Debate 5

Debate 5

Experiments on animals

Paragraph 4

However, since vivisection seems to be **regarded** as a necessary evil and there is a **notable reluctance** amongst medical researchers to **explore** alternative and **cruelty-free** methods of research, this **leads** us to the next question: 'Can such experiments on animals at least provide **tangible** results?' The answer to this question seems to be: '**Evidently** not.' The **overwhelming** weight of evidence would seem to **suggest** that drugs tested safely on animals and given the **green light** to go ahead in pharmaceutical production of drugs for human use often prove over time to be **fatal** or **detrimental** to humans. Thalidomide, a drug used in the 60s to prevent **morning sickness** that tested safe on animals but led to shocking **deformities** in humans, is such a **case in point**. So **blinded** were scientists, though, by the need to test on animals and **procure** only **acceptable** results through vivisection alone that they failed to **recall** the drug until it was shown that it caused birth **defects** in an animal model.

Vocabulary Building

Exercise A: Choose the option (**a**, **b**, **c** or **d**) which fits best each sentence.

1. I can only accept …….. evidence of his innocence; nothing less.

    a. tangible
    c. blinded
    b. detrimental
    d. notable

2. I'm afraid she has suffered a(n) ………. stroke.

    a. cruelty-free
    c. acceptable
    b. overwhelming
    d. fatal

Exercise B: Fill in the blanks in the following sentences using the correct form of the words from the box below. There are 2 extra words in the box you do not need to use.

a. regard	**b.** explore	**c.** lead	**d.** suggest	**e.** procure	**f.** recall

1. …Procuring…… food and other daily necessities was difficult.
2. He ……suggested…… an alternative solution to the company's problem that seemed reasonable.
3. The young prince was looking forward to ……leading…… his new army.
4. The manager is now……recalling…… all employees that have been laid off.

Exercise C: Fill in the definitions using words from the box below. There are 2 extra words in the box that you do not need to use.

a. reluctance	**b.** green light	**c.** morning sickness	**d.** defect	**e.** deformity	**f.** case in point

1. …Deformity…… is an acquired or congenital distortion of a bodily organ.
2. …Case in point…… means an example which shows that what one is saying is true.
3. …Green light…… refers to permission to proceed with a project.
4. …Reluctance…… is a lack of eagerness or willingness.

Exercise D: Fill in the chart with the derivatives of the given adjectives or adverbs. Then, provide one **synonym** and one **antonym**, taking into account their meaning in the specific text above.

	Verb	Noun	Adjective	Adverb
1.	note/notice	note/notableness/notice	notable	notably
2.	accept	acceptance	acceptable	acceptably
3.	evidence	evidence	evident	evidently
4.	-	detriment	detrimental	detrimentally

		Synonym	Antonym
1.	notable	noticable/striking	hidden/unknown
2.	acceptable	adequate/sufficient	unacceptable/poor
3.	evidently	obviously	vaguely/unclearly
4.	detrimental	harmful/damaging	beneficial/positive

Exercise E: Write 4 sentences using the following words: unacceptable, unknown, vaguely, beneficial. You must write 1 sentence for each of these words. Use between 8 and 15 words in each sentence.

(Suggested Answers)

1. Your behavior can only be seen as completely unacceptable.
2. There might be other unknown sides to this mystery.
3. He answered one of the questions rather vaguely.
4. The beneficial effects of a healthy diet are evident.

Experiments on animals

Paragraph 4

However, since vivisection seems to be regarded as a necessary evil and there is a notable reluctance amongst medical researchers to explore alternative and cruelty-free methods of research, this leads us to the next question: 'Can such experiments on animals at least provide **tangible** results?' **A** The answer to this question seems to be: 'Evidently not.' The overwhelming weight of evidence would seem to suggest that drugs tested safely on animals and given the green light to go ahead in pharmaceutical production of drugs for human use often prove over time to be fatal or detrimental to humans. **B** Thalidomide, a drug used in the 60s to prevent morning sickness that tested safe on animals, but led to shocking deformities in humans, is such a case in point. **C** So blinded were scientists, though, by the need to test on animals and procure only acceptable results through vivisection alone that they failed to recall the drug until it was shown that it caused birth defects in an animal model. **D**

Reading Comprehension

1. The word **tangible** in §4 is closest in meaning to
   a. incredible.
   b. demonstrable.
   c. sufficient.
   d. disputable.

2. According to the passage, what can be said of animal research?
   a. Research on animals produces consistent and credible results.
   b. It is a justifiable but unpleasant exercise.
   c. It has little relevance to humans.
   d. It has produced many invaluable drugs.

3. Why does the author make a reference to the drug Thalidomide?
   a. to underline the importance of animal research
   b. to discredit vivisection
   c. to warn against the use of pharmaceutical drugs
   d. to show how much scientific research has advanced since the sixties

4. Which sentence below expresses the essential information in the underlined sentence in §4?
   a. Blinkered vision led scientists to ignore the very evidence before their eyes.
   b. Scientists favor drug testing on humans over vivisection.
   c. Abnormalities in human pregnancies led scientists to take action.
   d. Scientists failed to make a connection between animal and human foetal deformities.

5. All of the following are true of the pharmaceutical industry **EXCEPT**
   a. the industry is over-reliant on animal research.
   b. drug defects do not immediately result in the recall of a drug.
   c. the industry loathes to introduce a new drug on the market, based alone on findings from animal research.
   d. drugs given the all-clear from animal testing are then released for human use.

6. Look at the four squares, **A**, **B**, **C** and **D**, which indicate where the following sentence could be added to the passage. Where would the sentence best fit? Right Answer: B

There are many such instances, but one is particularly notorious.

7. Select the appropriate sentences from the answer choices and match them to the relationship between drug testing on animals and the effect of drugs on humans. **TWO** of the answer choices will **NOT** be used. **This question is worth 3 points.**

   a. They could cause human foetal abnormalities.
   b. Scientists disregard initial side-effects of drugs.
   c. Drugs proved safe are considered acceptable for pharmaceutical distribution.
   d. Scientists are convinced of the validity of research findings.
   e. Side-effects are always predictable.
   f. Testing is often carried out over a lengthy period.
   g. Unexpected side-effects are possible.

Drug testing on animals:	C/D
Effect of drugs on humans:	A/B/G

Experiments on animals

Paragraph 5

Not only though, can 'safe' drugs procured through vivisection prove **positively harmful** to humans but the very **process** of vivisection itself is more **likely** to be **hindering** medical advances instead of helping them. Time spent on animal experiments would be better deployed on human studies, which **ultimately prove** more **effective**. It was human and not animal testing, for example, that **highlighted** the relationship between smoking and **lung** cancer and between diet and **colon** cancer. Furthermore, most medical **breakthroughs** have been **initiated** not by studies on animals but by **autopsy** and **clinical studies** on humans according to research. Even the **Physicians Committee** for **Responsible** Medicine (1998) has **issued** the **statement** that 'The **progress** of science is slowed **considerably** as money, that could be better spent on clinical studies and the **development** of more **reliable** in vitro studies, is **wasted** on animal tests.'

Vocabulary Building

Exercise A: Choose the option (**a**, **b**, **c** or **d**) which fits best each sentence.

1. The jet engine was a major .... in air transport.
   a. process
   b. breakthrough
   c. development
   d. progress

2. The company's revenue has increased ....
   a. ultimately
   b. positively
   c. likely
   d. considerably

Exercise B: Fill in the blanks in the following sentences using words from the box. You may need to change the word. There are 2 extra words in the box you do not need to use.

a. hinder	b. prove	c. highlight	d. initiate	e. issue	f. waste

1. I think it is time to ......initiate...... major social reforms.
2. The progress of our project is being ....hindered...... at the moment due to a lack of staff.
3. Recently conducted research highlights/has highlighted the problems that have emerged in the market.
4. He delayed ....issuing........ his book for another two months.

Exercise C: Fill in the definitions using words from the box below. There are 2 extra words in the box that you do not need to use.

a. physician	b. autopsy	c. clinical study	d. committee	e. colon	f. lung

1. ......Comittee...... means a group of people officially delegated to perform a function.
2. ......Autopsy...... is a medical examination of a dead body to determine the cause of death.
3. ...Clinical study... means a rigorously controlled test of a new drug on human subjects.
4. ......Physician...... is a person licensed to practice medicine.

Exercise D: Fill in the chart with the derivatives of the given adjectives or adverbs. Then, provide one **synonym** and one **antonym**, taking into account their meaning in the specific text above.

	Verb	Noun	Adjective	Adverb
1.	-	responsibility	responsible	responsibly
2.	rely	reliability	reliable	reliably
3.	harm	harm	harmful	harmfully
4.	affect	effect	effective	effectively

		Synonym	Antonym
1.	responsible	honorable/principled	irresponsible/untrustworthy
2.	reliable	trustworthy	unreliable
3.	harmful	detrimental	harmless
4.	effective	efficient/useful	insufficient/inadequate

Exercise E: Write 4 sentences using the following words: unreliable, harmless, irresponsible, inadequate. You must write 1 sentence for each of these words. Use between 8 and 15 words in each sentence.

(Suggested Answers)

1. The police is at a loss since all witnesses are believed to be unreliable.
2. No drug can be considered to be harmless as they all have side-effects.
3. You can under no circumstances trust such an irresponsible person.
4. The detective believes that such evidence is inadequate to accuse him of murder.

Debate 5

Experiments on animals

Paragraph 5

Not only though, can 'safe' drugs procured through vivisection prove positively harmful to humans, but the very process of vivisection itself is more likely to be **hindering** medical advances instead of helping them. **A** Time spent on animal experiments would be better deployed on human studies, which ultimately prove more effective. **B** It was human and not animal testing, for example, that highlighted the relationship between smoking and lung cancer and between diet and colon cancer. **C** Furthermore, most medical breakthroughs have been initiated not by studies on animals but by autopsy and clinical studies on humans according to research. Even the Physicians Committee for Responsible Medicine (1998) has issued the statement that 'The progress of science is slowed considerably as money, that could be better spent on clinical studies and the development of more reliable in vitro studies, is wasted on animal tests.' **D**

Reading Comprehension

1. The word **hindering** in §5 is closest in meaning to
   a. promoting.   c. perplexing.
   b. obstructing.   d. facilitating.

2. Based on the passage, how do respected medical bodies view animal research?
   a. with skepticism
   b. they reserve judgment
   c. with respect
   d. they exhibit indifference

3. Why does the author refer to the relationship between certain habits and diseases?
   a. to show that authorities monitor animal research
   b. to indicate the support of certain authorities for vivisection
   c. as a way of underlining the futility of animal research
   d. as a way of showing that ultimately animal research is an indispensable tool

4. Which sentence below best expresses the essential information in the underlined sentence in §5?
   a. Research on humans is to be credited mostly for advances in medicine.
   b. Human guinea pigs acting as live subjects in drug testing alone produce valid data.
   c. Findings in research on humans has been validated by vivisection.
   d. Research on humans has rarely yielded valid data.

5. All of the following are true of current pharmaceutical knowledge **EXCEPT**
   a. without animal testing no significant results could ever have been achieved.
   b. valuable resources are being expended needlessly on vivisection.
   c. humans, too, have played a significant role in medical progress.
   d. various authorities question the validity of animal research.

6. Look at the four squares, **A**, **B**, **C** and **D**, which indicate where the following sentence could be added to the passage. Where would the sentence best fit?   Right Answer: D

   Such a declaration must count for something.

7. Select the appropriate sentences from the answer choices and match them to the relationship between human and animal tests. **TWO** of the answer choices will **NOT** be used. **This question is worth 3 points.**

   a. They divert valuable resources from more valid forms of testing.
   b. A link has been demonstrated between illness and lifestyle choices.
   c. Dissection has yielded valuable information.
   d. Tests impede medical progress.
   e. They are designed to be infallible.
   f. Little valid information is ever revealed from such tests.
   g. Time has proved the validity of such tests.

Human tests:	B/C
Animal tests:	A/D/F

Experiments on animals

Paragraph 6

So, given the hopelessly **outdated** methodology, as well as **possibly perilous outcomes** of animal experiments used for drug testing, there can be no **justifiable grounds** whatsoever for arguing in favor of this barbaric and **antiquated practice**. Even more so, when experiments on humans have produced drugs that are safer to use than a lot of those **developed** through animal experiments. In addition, **recent** advances in **stem cell** research in the not-so-**distant**-future will largely **obviate** the need for any **exploitation** of animals. However, as long as governments **see fit** to fund vivisection, the day when alternative methods of research will replace animal testing will still **remain** on the distant horizon. Meanwhile, **countless** animals continue to die in pain, **needlessly**, as funds are **diverted** into the **abominable** practice of vivisection that **masquerades** as 'science.' We must act now to put an end to this.

Vocabulary Building

Exercise A: Choose the option (**a**, **b**, **c** or **d**) which fits best each sentence.

1. The family reunion brought up .... memories.
   a. recent   **c.** antiquated
   b. outdated   **d. distant**

2. The union is protesting against the .... treatment of prisoners.
   a. justifiable   **c. abominable**
   b. countless   **d.** perilous

Exercise B: Fill in the blanks in the following sentences using words from the box. You may need to change the word. There are 2 extra words in the box you do not need to use.

a. develop	**b.** obviate	**c.** see fit	**d.** divert	**e.** remain	**f.** masquerade

1. We are optimistic that this will ...... obviate ...... the need for an operation.
2. The traffic warden was ...... diverting ...... the traffic around the scene of the accident.
3. A cure still ...... remains ...... to be found.
4. She ...... developed ...... her argument in a series of articles she published.

Exercise C: Fill in the definitions using words from the box below. There are 2 extra words in the box that you do not need to use.

a. outcome	**b.** ground	**c.** practice	**d.** stem cell	**e.** exploitation

1. ...... Exploitation ...... means an act of employing something to the greatest possible advantage.
2. ...... Outcome ...... is something that follows from an action; an end result.
3. ...... Practice ...... refers to a usual or customary action.

Exercise D: Fill in the chart with the derivatives of the given adjectives or adverbs. Then, provide one **synonym** and one **antonym**, taking into account their meaning in the specific text above.

	Verb	Noun	Adjective	Adverb
1.	-	possibility	possible	possibly
2.	need	need	needless/needy	needlessly
3.	count	counting/counter	countless	countlessly
4.	(im)peril	peril	perilous	perilously

		Synonym	Antonym
1.	possibly	probably	impossibly/improbably
2.	needlessly	pointlessly	necessarily
3.	countless	innumerable/immeasurable	limited/few
4.	perilous	dangerous/threatening	harmless/innocent

Exercise E: Write 4 sentences using the following words: innocent, necessarily, impossibly, limited. You must write 1 sentence for each of these words. Use between 8 and 15 words in each sentence. (Suggested Answers)

1. They initially thought of it as an innocent prank.
2. I think that you necessarily have to accept the offer.
3. This operation was thought to be impossibly difficult but not any more.
4. We will try to proceed with the limited resources available.

Debate 5

Experiments on animals

Paragraph 6

So, given the hopelessly outdated methodology, as well as possibly perilous outcomes of animal experiments used for drug testing, there can be no justifiable grounds whatsoever for arguing in favor of this barbaric and antiquated practice. **A** Even more so, when experiments on humans have produced drugs that are safer to use than a lot of those developed through animal experiments. In addition, recent advances in stem cell research in the not-so-distant-future will largely obviate the need for any experimentation on animals. However, as long as governments see fit to fund vivisection, the day when alternative methods of research will replace animal testing will still remain on the distant horizon. **B** Meanwhile, countless animals continue to die in pain, needlessly, as funds are diverted into the abominable practice of vivisection that **masquerades** as 'science.' **C** We must act now to put an end to this. **D**

Reading Comprehension

1. The word **masquerades** in §6 is closest in meaning to
   a. feigns.
   b. exemplifies.
   c. discredits.
   d. ridicules.

2. Based on the passage, what can be said of the future of animal testing?
   a. It is temporarily secure but things might change.
   b. It may gain in popularity.
   c. It will prove more valid than human testing.
   d. It will prove indispensable.

3. What does the author believe is the biggest obstacle in dispensing with animal testing?
   a. indifference to the animals themselves
   b. its sound methodology
   c. lack of other possible alternatives
   d. inadequate financial support for alternative forms of testing

4. Which sentence below best expresses the essential information in the underlined sentences in §6?
   a. Animal testing can yield drugs developed through tried-and-tested methodology.
   b. Drugs obtained through animal testing are potentially unsafe, due to archaic methodology.
   c. Animal experiments can seriously endanger the lives of animals, which is unforgivable.
   d. Animal research is built upon years of scientific experiments, which whilst cruel, are valuable for medical progress.

5. All of the following are mentioned by the author as a future possibility **EXCEPT**
   a. stem cell research could replace vivisection.
   b. pain-free experiments on animals will be devised.
   c. funding will still be channeled into vivisection.
   d. animal experiments will become obsolete.

6. Look at the four squares, **A**, **B**, **C** and **D**, which indicate where the following sentence could be added to the passage. Where would the sentence best fit?   Right Answer: A

   Despite advocates of vivisection protesting otherwise.

7. Select the appropriate sentences from the answer choices and match them to the relationship between the alternative methods to animal testing and animal testing. **TWO** of the answer choices will **NOT** be used. **This question is worth 3 points.**

   a. They have made no impact on the field of medicine.
   b. In some areas, they are still a work in progress.
   c. The methodology of such testing is anachronistic.
   d. They are difficult to justify on many grounds.
   e. Funding is inadequate.
   f. Progress is proving slower than expected.
   g. They receive little public support.

Alternative methods to animal testing:	B/E/F
Animal testing:	C/D

Vivisection is a Positive Thing, too

Debate 5

Paragraph 1

Without doubt, vivisection is a highly emotive issue. The fact that cute and **endearing** animals, such as kittens and rabbits, which are often the beloved pets of our childhood, are frequently employed in animal experiments serves to further **polarize** the anti and pro sides of the vivisection debate. The thought that such weak and defenseless animals are **subjected** to often **agonizing** drug tests is hard to stomach. However, no advance in medicine or technology was ever made without some form of **sacrifice**. Astonishing and **rapid** advances in the field of medicine, can be **directly** traced back to successful drug tests on animals, so surely this is no time for **squeamishness** or pontificating about the rights of animals. After all, don't humans also have rights? The right to a healthy and disease-free life?

Paragraph 2

Advances in medicine that we now take for **granted**, such as antibiotics, blood **transfusions**, **vaccines** or asthma medication would not have been possible without animal research. Although **cell** and **tissue** culture research is advancing rapidly and **generating** answers to medical conundrums hitherto unsolved, there are still some grey areas that only animal research can **adequately** resolve. It would be **ludicrous** now to put an end to animal research having come so far and made so many discoveries that will greatly **enhance** our lives. Who in all honesty, after all, would refuse vital medicine if they were seriously ill, just because the medicine had been tested previously on animals?

Paragraph 3

Those against animal research have argued that humans could replace animals in some experiments with human guinea pigs. Firstly, it is **questionable** if the proponents of this argument would put their money where their mouth is and **volunteer** themselves for such experiments. However, that aside, how ethical would such experiments be, if we consider that humans are **arguably** of more value than animals? Is it really justifiable to **induce** cancer in a human when mice can be **bred purely** for the purpose of animal research and hence are more **dispensable** than humans? Also, those who **advocate** the use of humans in medical research surely cannot have forgotten the **hideous** outcome of one **infamous** drug testing program on human volunteers that had such **devastating** consequences on the participants that it became **notorious** and is now known as the 'elephant man drug trial' on account of the fact that the heads of the human volunteers swelled to the size of an elephant's head, within seconds of being administered the drug. Who, given the unpredictability of trial drugs would insist on their being tested on humans?

Paragraph 4

Another argument against vivisection is the cruelty to animals involved in animal research. However, have any of the opponents of vivisection ever stopped to think about the rampant cruelty that is in evident daily, in the meat industry? Animals, such as battery hens are kept in **appalling** conditions for weeks on end and suffer just as much stress and **discomfort** as laboratory animals. Ironically, laboratory animals are probably given a much better deal than those **destined** for the meat industry, as there are strict procedures and measures that must be followed in the treatment of the **former**. In addition, once animals are of no further use in medical research, they are humanely killed, in contrast to the barbaric end that meets animals destined for the **slaughterhouse**. Moreover, 1600 animals, **predominantly** chickens, are slaughtered every second worldwide for the meat industry, which makes the relatively small number of animals killed in the laboratory, seem pale by comparison.

Paragraph 5

In conclusion, it would seem that vivisection is no more cruel a **practice** than breeding and slaughtering animals for food. Like the meat industry, vivisection is a necessary evil, without which we would still be living in the Dark Ages of medical science, at the **mercy** of **microbes** that hitherto would have caused unnecessary suffering and often death, but which we can now **largely overcome** with the use of antibiotics. It is **utter** hypocrisy to **condemn** the practice of vivisection, while making use of the **fruits** of animal research, in the form of palliatives and cures for illness. With regard to animal testing, it could be said that in such a case, the end very much justifies the means and those who would beg to disagree are either blind to the truth or just pure hypocrites.

Vocabulary Building

Exercise A: Choose the option (**a**, **b**, **c** or **d**) which fits best each sentence.

1. His family was subjected to a(n) .... attack.
   a. infamous   **c. hideous**
   b. notorious   d. questionable

2. The minister said the reforms would .... new jobs.
   a. subject   **c. generate**
   b. induce   d. polarize

3. Gym fees range from inexpensive to ....
   a. agonizing   c. appalling
   b. devastating   **d. ludicrous**

4. A new anti-malaria .... is now undergoing trials.
   a. vaccine   c. cell
   b. transfusion   d. tissue

5. The landscape has remained .... rural in appearance.
   a. adequately   **c. predominantly**
   b. arguably   d. largely

6. She was in .... denial after her husband's death.
   a. utter   c. granted
   b. former   d. rapid

Exercise B: Fill in the blanks in the following sentences using words from the box. You may need to change the word. There are 2 extra words in the box you do not need to use.

a. polarize	b. enhance	c. volunteer	d. breed	e. advocate	f. destine	g. overcome	h. condemn

1. Everyone should ......condemn...... racism.
2. The protesters will continue ......advocating...... higher salaries for workers.
3. Our company has already ......enhanced...... its reputation abroad.
4. Doctors always ...volunteer...... their services very willingly.
5. He was determined to ......overcome...... all difficulties.
6. I'm afraid your foolish scheme is ......destined...... to fail.

Exercise C: Fill in the definitions using words from the box below. There are 2 extra words in the box that you do not need to use.

a. sacrifice	b. squeamishness	c. discomfort	d. slaughterhouse	e. practice	f. mercy	g. microbe	h. fruit

1. ......Slaughterhouse...... is a place where animals are butchered.
2. ......Discomfort...... means mental or bodily distress.
3. ......Fruit...... means result; outcome.
4. ......Sacrifice...... is a surrender of something of value as a means of gaining something else.
5. ......Squimishness...... means shock and disgust.
6. ......Microbe...... is a microscopic organism, such as a disease-causing bacterium.

Exercise D: Fill in the chart with the derivatives of the given adjectives or adverbs. Then, provide one **synonym** and one **antonym**, taking into account their meaning in the specific text above.

	Verb	Noun	Adjective	Adverb
1.	direct	direction/directness	direct/directional	directly
2.	purify	purity	pure	purely
3.	endear	endearment	endearing	endearingly
4.	agonize	agony	agonizing	agonizingly
5.	devastate	devastation	devastating	devastatingly
6.	dispense	dispense/-ibility	dispensable	dispensably

		Synonym	Antonym
1.	directly	immediately/definitely	indirectly
2.	purely	entirely/solely	partly/partially
3.	endearing	adorable/lovable	unlovable
4.	agonizing	tortuous/unbearable	pleasant/enjoyable
5.	devastating	adverse/unfavorable	favorable/fortunate
6.	dispensable	expendable/disposable	essential/indispensable

Exercise E: Write 6 sentences using the following words: partially, essential, unlovable, fortunate, indirectly, pleasant. You must write 1 sentence for each of these words. Use between 8 and 15 words in each sentence.

(Suggested Answers)

1. She had an accident when she was 18 and is now partially blind.
2. It is essential that all passengers remain in their seats during take-off.
3. He is such an unlovable man that even his family has abandoned him.
4. It was a fortunate coincidence that we met here tonight.
5. He indirectly suggested that I should reconsider my offer.
6. Traveling abroad was more than a pleasant experience for our family.

Debate 5

TOEFL Exam Practice: Reading Comprehension

Debate 5

Paragraph 1

Without doubt, vivisection is a highly emotive issue. The fact that cute and endearing animals, such as kittens and rabbits, which are often the beloved pets of our childhood, are frequently employed in animal experiments serves to further polarize the anti and pro sides of the vivisection debate. The thought that such weak and defenseless animals are subjected to often agonizing drug tests is **hard to stomach**. However, no advance in medicine or technology was ever made without some form of sacrifice. Astonishing and rapid advances in the field of medicine, can be directly traced back to successful drug tests on animals, so surely this is no time for squeamishness or **pontificating** about the rights of animals. After all, don't humans also have rights? The right to a healthy and disease-free life?

1. The phrase **hard to stomach** in §1 is closest in meaning to
   a. difficult to dispute.
   c. difficult to accept.
   b. a source of pain.
   d. a sadistic act.

2. The word **pontificating** in §1 is closest in meaning to
   a. protesting.
   c. analyzing.
   b. deliberating.
   d. decreeing.

3. Based on the passage, what effect do domestic pets have on the vivisection debate?
   a. They dissuade people from supporting vivisection.
   b. They make vivisection seem more unreal as we identify with our pets.
   c. They serve to divide opinion more forcefully.
   d. They make those conducting animal tests seem less callous and uncaring.

Paragraph 2

Advances in medicine that we now take for granted, such as antibiotics, blood transfusions, vaccines or asthma medication would not have been possible without animal research. Although cell and tissue culture research is advancing rapidly and generating answers to medical **conundrums** hitherto unsolved, there are still some grey areas that only animal research can adequately resolve. It would be ludicrous now to put an end to animal research having come so far and made so many discoveries that will greatly enhance our lives. Who in all honesty, after all, would refuse vital medicine if they were seriously ill, just because the medicine had been tested previously on animals?

4. The word **conundrums** in §2 is closest in meaning to
   a. puzzles.
   b. difficulties.
   c. absurdities.
   d. discrepancies.

5. What does the author believe is true of animal experimentation?
   a. It is in a unique position to shed light on medical science.
   b. There are aspects of it that are rather hazy.
   c. It is more sophisticated than alternative methods of testing.
   d. Alternative methods of testing will overshadow it in the future.

Paragraph 3

Those against animal research have argued that humans could replace animals in some experiments with human guinea pigs. Firstly, it is questionable if the **proponents** of this argument would put their money where their mouth is and volunteer themselves for such experiments. However, that aside, how ethical would such experiments be, if we consider that humans are arguably of more value than animals? Is it really justifiable to induce cancer in a human when mice can be bred purely for the purpose of animal research and hence are more dispensable than humans? Also, those who advocate the use of humans in medical research surely cannot have forgotten the hideous outcome of one infamous drug testing program on human volunteers that had such devastating consequences on the participants that it became notorious and is now known as the 'elephant man drug trial' on account of the fact that the heads of the human volunteers swelled to the size of an elephant's head, within seconds of being administered the drug. Who, given the unpredictability of trial drugs would insist on their being tested on humans?

6. The word **proponents** in §3 is closest in meaning to
   a. advocates.
   b. deriders.
   c. debaters.
   d. theorists.

7. What does the author believe is morally reprehensible?
   a. Human volunteers are not forthcoming.
   b. There is a failure to vet human guinea-pigs before testing
   c. Inadequate testing measures exist for human testing.
   d. Animals should be placed on equal footing with humans.

8. Select the appropriate sentences from the answer choices and match them to the relationship between animal testing and human testing. **TWO** of the answer choices will **NOT** be used. **This question is worth 3 points.**

   a. The experimental subjects are dispensable commodities.
   b. Some experiments have achieved lasting notoriety.
   c. Some experimental subjects might consciously decide not to participate.
   d. There should be limits imposed on what experimental subjects should be subjected to.
   e. The future of such testing hangs in the balance.
   f. There is no shortage of volunteers for medical drug trials.
   g. Experimental subjects only exist to be experimented on.

Animal testing:	A/G
Human testing:	B/C/D

Paragraph 4

Another argument against vivisection is the cruelty to animals involved in animal research. However, have any of the opponents of vivisection ever stopped to think about the **rampant** cruelty that is in evident daily, in the meat industry? Animals, such as battery hens are kept in appalling conditions for weeks on end and suffer just as much stress and discomfort as laboratory animals. Ironically, laboratory animals are probably given a much better deal than those destined for the meat industry, as there are strict procedures and measures that must be followed in the treatment of the former. In addition, once animals are of no further use in medical research, they are humanely killed-in contrast to the barbaric end that meets animals destined for the slaughterhouse. Moreover, 1600 animals-predominantly chickens-are slaughtered every second worldwide, for the meat industry, which makes the relatively small number of animals killed in the laboratory, seem **pale by comparison.**

9. The word **rampant** in §4 is closest in meaning to
   a. unrestricted.   c. sadistict.
   b. controversial.   d. thoughtless.

10. What is the difference, according to the author, between animals bred for the meat industry and those bred for animal research?
   a. Animals bred for research live longer.
   b. Animals destined for the meat industry get a comparatively raw deal.

   c. Animals bred for meat are treated with more compassion.
   d. Research animals are inhumanely killed.

11. The phrase **pale by comparison** in §4 is closest in meaning to
   a. significantly shocking.
   b. relatively unimportant.
   c. remarkable.
   d. unjustifiable.

Paragraph 5

Ⓐ In conclusion, it would seem that vivisection is no more cruel a practice than breeding and slaughtering animals for food. Ⓑ Like the meat industry, vivisection is a necessary evil, without which we would still be living in the Dark Ages of medical science, at the mercy of microbes that hitherto would have caused unnecessary suffering and often death, but which we can now largely overcome with the use of antibiotics. Ⓒ It is utter hypocrisy to condemn the practice of vivisection, while making use of the fruits of animal research, in the form of **palliatives** and cures for illness. With regard to animal testing, it could be said that in such a case, the end very much justifies the means and those who would beg to disagree are either blind to the truth or just pure hypocrites. Ⓓ

12. The word **palliatives** in §5 is closest in meaning to
   a. relievers.
   b. remedies.
   c. eradicators.
   d. restorers.

13. The author has the opinion that
   a. opponents of vivisection, at least have the courage of their convictions.
   b. research animals are not as well treated as those bred for meat.
   c. the introduction of antibiotics, rather than animal experimentation has alleviated human suffering.
   d. animal suffering in vivisection is grossly exaggerated.

14. Look at the four squares, Ⓐ, Ⓑ, Ⓒ and Ⓓ, which indicate where the following sentence could be added to the passage. Where would the sentence best fit?   Right Answer: C

We should be grateful for such advances, irrespective of the means by which such progress was initially accomplished.

VOCABULARY: Revision Multiple Choice Questions

Vocabulary Revision

1. Policies don't .... the sheer number of tests.
   a. enable
   b. disregard
   c. contend
   d. mandate

2. Some experts have made persuasive .... for how emphasis on test scores has commodified education.
   a. chats
   b. arguments
   c. causes
   d. approaches

3. Under the .... circumstances, schools may well become nothing more than test-preparation centers.
   a. current
   b. coming
   c. desirable
   d. distant

4. Standardized tests make teachers .... for their students' performance.
   a. dispensable
   b. esteemed
   c. accountable
   d. experienced

5. .... of standardized tests also contend that these exams can only measure superficial concepts.
   a. Detractors
   b. Methods
   c. Peers
   d. Professionals

6. Tests indicate when teachers need to .... their approach.
   a. recommend
   b. sideline
   c. research
   d. adjust

7. She found these results particularly ....
   a. intriguing
   b. skeptical
   c. tailored
   d. undeveloped

8. The trend .... that people have adopted online educational offerings.
   a. undertakes
   b. reflects
   c. accelerates
   d. attributes

9. The considered online forms of education are difficult to ....
   a. capitalize
   b. conform
   c. negotiate
   d. decode

10. The role of teachers should .... merely instructing academic subject matters.
    a. demonstrate
    b. divert
    c. enable
    d. transcend

VOCABULARY: Revision Multiple Choice Questions

11. The Academy has established itself as a ……. provider of educational lessons.
   a. existing
   b. high
   c. likely
   d. leading

12. This flexibility is especially ………. to mid-career professionals.
   a. attractive
   b. outdated
   c. perilous
   d. current

13. Apple is a place where college graduates ………. .
   a. devote
   b. embolden
   c. thrive
   d. preserve

14. Online education, ……….., may not be an alternative solution to learning.
   a. professionally
   b. ultimately
   c. relatively
   d. especially

15. Uniforms often cause ………. during the day.
   a. distractions
   b. evaluations
   c. feedback
   d. guidelines

16. Worrying about uniforms is just another ………. of discomfort.
   a. grade
   b. line
   c. piece
   d. layer

17. I think ………. school uniforms will be a huge step.
   a. processing
   b. reasoning
   c. eliminating
   d. recommending

18. Children are not careful about ………. the quality of their clothes.
   a. preserving
   b. replacing
   c. suppressing
   d. transforming

19. A tie and a blazer were not my ………. wardrobe choices.
   a. unconventional
   b. ideal
   c. unique
   d. granted

20. I ………. with those experts who contend uniforms reduce distraction.
   a. concur
   b. gear
   c. initiate
   d. trumpet

VOCABULARY: Revision Multiple Choice Questions

21. Many schools have ………. suppliers and outlets.
  a. undertaken
  b. yielded
  c. recommended
  d. mandated

22. I want my kids to ………. in life and thus, I believe, school uniforms are the best thing.
  a. judge
  b. invest
  c. hinder
  d. excel

23. Few would ………. the incredible advances made in the field of medical research.
  a. illustrate
  b. improve
  c. measure
  d. dispute

24. Finding a cure for these diseases would be a(n) ………. .
  a. game changer
  b. pride
  c. remark
  d. advance

25. It was shown that the drug caused birth ………. .
  a. sentiments
  b. emergencies
  c. defects
  d. functions

26. Funds are diverted to the ………. practice of vivisection.
  a. perilous
  b. abominable
  c. human
  d. ludicrous

27. Defenseless animals are ………. to agonizing drug tests.
  a. subjected
  b. nurtured
  c. participated
  d. accredited

28. An infamous drug testing program had ………. consequences on the participants.
  a. agonizing
  b. determining
  c. enriching
  d. devastating

29. Animals are held in appalling ………. for weeks.
  a. consequences
  b. conditions
  c. circumstances
  d. communities

30. It is utter hypocrisy to ………. vivisection when making use of the fruits of animal research.
  a. exceed
  b. induce
  c. condemn
  d. underestimate

VOCABULARY: Revision Multiple Choice Questions

31. Researchers have ………. the validity of children learning music.
   a. debated
   b. accredited
   c. capitalized
   d. distinguished

32. One of the skills music enhances is the ability to ………. language.
   a. embolden
   b. employ
   c. form
   d. acquire

33. Playing an instrument ………. requires a person to use more of their brain.
   a. individually
   b. ironically
   c. essentially
   d. markedly

34. The benefits of music education have been made ………. in standardized test performance.
   a. notorious
   b. evident
   c. outdated
   d. popular

35. My son participates in three ………. classes per week.
   a. prestigious
   b. extracurricular
   c. relevant
   d. seasonal

36. Such classes provide children with a(n) ………. in school.
   a. side-effect
   b. trait
   c. advantage
   d. value

37. The performing arts instill values of patience and ………. .
   a. discipline
   b. unity
   c. sentiment
   d. remark

38. It is important for children to be exposed to a(n) ………. of activities.
   a. quality
   b. variety
   c. portion
   d. opportunity

39. She has been fighting the ………. dominance of standardized testing.
   a. lucrative
   b. invaluable
   c. emerging
   d. innovative

40. The complete discussion ………. around how to raise test scores.
   a. revolves
   b. grows
   c. forms
   d. establishes

Vocabulary Revision

Debate 6

Obesity: Should Schools and Governments Intervene?

Such is the all-consuming, if you pardon the pun, issue of obesity that everyone from politicians to high-profile celebrities has waded into the imbroglio. The New York mayor has forced food outlets to display calorific contents of meals on menus, whilst the British Prime Minister has called for an end to the 'moral neutrality' of not passing judgement on obesity. Fellow Brit comedian, Ricky Gervais, nailed the prevailing anti-fat hysteria in his comment on obesity: 'Fat equals thick, fat equals lack of control and overeating, fat equals poverty and moral bankruptcy, a potent combination of social and bodily hatred.' These messages are but the tip of the iceberg of the underlying miasma of hate that pervades society's attitude toward the obese, outrageously displayed on one San Francisco billboard outside a gym that depicted an alien, the underlying caption being 'When they come, they'll eat the fat ones first.'

Riding on the wave of the obesity hysteria, schools and governments are now intervening to try and reverse the obesity trend. After having been bombarded by food fascists with the message of 'five a day' referring to our required vegetable/fruit intake, we are now being told to achieve a certain BMI (Body Mass Index) compatible with our height/age and gender. But by what criteria are the 'higher authorities' determining our optimum BMI? Just one look at European Art over the centuries, depicting bodies that would seem grossly overweight to today's society - take Renoir's fleshy, voluptuous women, as one case in point - illustrate how society's definition of what is 'obese' and therefore unhealthy and unattractive varies wildly according to the age. Cross-culturally too, obese is beautiful in some African cultures, like Nigeria's Efik community. To be called a 'slim princess' is the ultimate slur on one's character. So much so, that young adolescent girls will spend months in forced inactivity, consuming a starch-rich diet to achieve optimum levels of rotundity, a tribal symbol of health and beauty. So by what authority can governments and schools dictate the ideal body shape to individuals, when cross-culturally and across the centuries, ideas of the perfect body are so greatly at variance with one another?

Such anti-obese hysteria and the necessity for government and school intervention, might even be justified, if there were some medical basis to it, assuming that is, that one could even adequately come up with a definition of what constitutes 'obese' in the first instance. Though even with regard to the obesity/health issue, the jury is still out. Obesity has been linked to illnesses as diverse as cardiovascular disease, diabetes and cancer. However, there is a growing backlash against this element of 'fatism' in society instigated by a small, but nonetheless, vociferous minority in the medical profession. Paul Campos, law professor and author of the 'Diet Myth', has even gone so far as to stick his neck out and question the link between obesity and mortality; a connection which has even been challenged by an article in the much-respected Journal of the American Medical Association (JAMA). Author of the aforesaid article, Katherine Flegal of the 'Center for Disease Control and Prevention' (CDC), calls the severity of the dangers of excess body fat into question, indicating that the number of overweight and obesity-related deaths is actually about 26,000, about one fifteenth the earlier estimate of 400,000.

Since it can be seen that obesity itself is hard to define and is erroneously linked to medical problems, it would seem that the intervention of authorities in the matter of obesity is not just intrusive but also groundless. Furthermore, even were there to be a proven link between illness and obesity and an ideal body shape to conform to, what right do authorities have to insist on taking control over an individual's life choices and lifestyle? An individual is by definition, just that. A free person with the right to make their own life choices even if it is to the detriment of their bodily shape/health. Infringement of such rights smacks of totalitarianism. Totalitarian regimes seek to control every aspect of an individual's life from religion to education. Controling an individual's dietary regime surely is just one step removed from a Big Brother-type scenario where the individual is but an automaton controlled by the state. Interestingly, Paul Campo made the point, in his eponymous book, that the intervention of authorities in the obesity issue is not so much motivated by health concerns as by an underlying hatred of society for the obese. Now, that one might say is real food for thought.

What really seems to be the issue therefore is that modern society finds obesity repulsive. This is the real reason behind anti-obesity campaigns. Fat people just seem to be air-brushed out of society. Any doubt that this should be the case is swiftly removed by a cursory glance at the glossy magazines on sale. When was the last time you saw an oversize model, oversize meaning size 8 and above, staring out at you from the magazine racks? Admittedly, Cosmopolitan made a brief incursion into the realm of the more 'generous sized' by displaying magazines with 'large' models and others with 'normal' models to see which magazine sold but this experiment was never repeated, presumably because 'large' doesn't sell. So it is we as a society that is at fault. If we change our perceptions, then maybe intervention on obesity will seem both irrelevant and unnecessary.

So it can be seen that government/school intervention cannot be justified at any level, from the purely aesthetic to the medical. At best it can be seen as meddling, but at worst a more sinister attempt of the state to infiltrate the individual's life and very being to ensure absolute power and control over the individuals themselves. It would be laughable were it not for the message that such governmental intervention is sending out to us all: 'We own you intellectually but physically, too.' Political issues aside, such body fascism just makes for a society that is paranoid and miserable about its bodily image, with the knock-on effects of a lowering of self-esteem leading to a plethora of other problems both psychological and physical, anorexia being just one such example. Isn't it time therefore that we made a stand against authoritarian meddling in our lives and became responsible for our own diet and daily exercise regimes? So, pass me the cream cakes please. Oh and while you're at it tear up that government leaflet on 'Healthy Eating' that's just dropped on my doormat.

Paragraph 1

Such is the all-consuming, if you pardon the pun, issue of obesity that everyone from politicians to high-profile celebrities have waded into the **imbroglio**. **A** The New York mayor has forced food outlets to display calorific contents of meals on menus, whilst the British Prime Minister has called for an end to the 'moral neutrality' of not passing judgement on obesity. **B** Fellow Brit comedian, Ricky Gervais, nailed the prevailing anti-fat hysteria in his comment on obesity: 'Fat equals thick, fat equals lack of control and overeating, fat equals poverty and moral bankruptcy, a potent combination of social and bodily hatred.' These messages are but the tip of the iceberg of the underlying miasma of hate that pervades society's attitude toward the obese. **C** Such an attitude was outrageously displayed on one billboard outside a gym that depicted an alien, the underlying caption being 'When they come, they'll eat the fat ones first.' **D**

Reading Comprehension

1. The word **imbroglio** in §1 is closest in meaning to
   a. muddle.
   b. controversy.
   c. argument.
   d. debate.

2. According to the passage what did Gervais achieve?
   a. He whipped up anti-fat hysteria.
   b. He called for an end to fat prejudice in society.
   c. He succinctly summed up society's stance on obesity.
   d. He managed to polarize public feeling in the obesity debate.

3. What does the author believe is true of the attitude of society to the obese?
   a. It is irrational.
   b. There is a degree of understanding.
   c. Overall an attitude of indifference prevails.
   d. Anti-obesity feeling is restricted to only a small minority.

4. Which sentence below best expresses the essential information in the underlined sentence in §1?
   a. Feelings of hatred for the obese have now peaked in society.
   b. Gervais' statement only reflects the views of a minority.
   c. The beliefs aired by Gervais are more modest than society's hatred of the obese.
   d. Society's hatred of the obese is nevertheless underpinned by a degree of tolerance.

5. All of the following are true of how obese are viewed in modern society **EXCEPT**
   a. they are considered intellectually inferior.
   b. there is a failure on the part of the obese to exert self-restraint.
   c. their weight is self-induced.
   d. excess size is linked to financial wealth.

6. Look at the four squares, **A**, **B**, **C** and **D**, which indicate where the following sentence could be added to the passage. Where would the sentence best fit?   Right Answer: D

   By and large, this is discrimination taken to entirely new heights.

7. An introductory sentence for a brief summary of the passage is provided below. Complete the summary by selecting the **THREE** answer choices that express the most important ideas in the passage. Some sentences do not belong in the summary because they express ideas that are not presented in the passage or are ideas of minor importance. **This question is worth 2 points.**

   People from all walks of life have become involved in the obesity debate.

   a. Certain politicians have taken active steps to curb obesity.
   b. Most politicians have taken outrageous stances in the obesity debate.
   c. Comedians have also praised the obese.
   d. Gervais's negative comments merely echoed society's take on the obese.
   e. Anti-obese attitudes are more deep-rooted in society than is immediately apparent.
   f. Gyms are now launching an anti-obese campaign.

Paragraph 2

<u>Riding on the wave of the obesity hysteria, schools and governments are now intervening to try and reverse the obesity trend.</u> After having been bombarded by food fascists with the message of 'five a day' referring to our required vegetable/fruit intake, we are now being told to achieve a certain BMI (Body Mass Index) compatible with our height/age and gender. **A** But by what criteria are the 'higher authorities' determining our optimum BMI? Just one look at European Art over the centuries, depicting bodies that would seem grossly overweight to today's society – take Renoir's fleshy, **voluptuous** women, as one case in point – illustrate how society's definition of what is 'obese' and therefore unhealthy and unattractive varies wildly according to the age. **B** Cross-culturally too, obese is beautiful in some African cultures, like Nigeria's Efik community. To be called a 'slim princess' is the ultimate slur on one's character. **C** So much so, that young adolescent girls will spend months in forced inactivity, consuming a starch-rich diet to achieve optimum levels of rotundity, a tribal symbol of health and beauty. **D** So by what authority can governments and schools dictate the ideal body shape to individuals, when cross-culturally and across the centuries, ideas of the perfect body are so greatly at variance with one another?

Reading Comprehension

1. The word **voluptuous** in §2 is closest in meaning to
   a. curvaceous.
   b. wanton.
   c. undisciplined.
   d. over-indulgent.

2. According to the passage, society's view of the ideal body shape is
   a. highly variable.
   b. consistent across cultures.
   c. immutable.
   d. logical.

3. What attitude does the author have toward authorities that intervene on body/weight issues?
   a. skepticism
   b. admiration
   c. annoyance
   d. tolerance

4. Which sentence below best expresses the essential information in the underlined sentence in §2?
   a. The intervention of authorities is undoing the good work done so far in tackling obesity.
   b. Authorities have been reluctant to change their attitude toward obesity.
   c. The spotlight on obesity in contemporary society has motivated authorities to act.
   d. Past attitudes of authorities toward obesity were verging on hysteria.

5. According to the passage, all of the following are true of the intervention of authorities on the issue of obesity **EXCEPT**
   a. it is uncalled for.
   b. it is groundless.
   c. it is heavy-handed.
   d. it is justified.

6. Look at the four squares, **A**, **B**, **C** and **D**, which indicate where the following sentence could be added to the passage. Where would the sentence best fit? Right Answer: A

   This is just a step too far.

7. An introductory sentence for a brief summary of the passage is provided below. Complete the summary by selecting the **THREE** answer choices that express the most important ideas in the passage. Some sentences do not belong in the summary because they express ideas that are not presented in the passage or are ideas of minor importance. **This question is worth 2 points.**

   Authorities are jumping on the anti-obesity bandwagon and trying to tackle obesity in society.

   a. Past intervention of authorities even extended to dictating people's diet.
   b. This intervention has been initially well-received.
   c. Current intervention by authorities has now extended beyond dictating diet to dictating ideal body shape.
   d. Renoir and other great artists were often criticized for their depiction of the female form.
   e. Bodily ideals vary so greatly across time and culture that it is pointless to strive for a bodily ideal.
   f. It is hoped that one day soon most people will conform to the bodily ideal.

Paragraph 3

Such anti-obese hysteria and the necessity for government and school intervention, might even be justified, if there were some medical basis to it, assuming that is, that one could even adequately come up with a definition of what constitutes 'obese' in the first instance. **A** Though even with regard to the obesity/health issue, the jury is still out. **B** Obesity has been linked to illnesses as diverse as cardiovascular disease, diabetes and cancer. However, there is a growing backlash against this element of 'fatism' in society instigated by a small, but nonetheless, **vociferous** minority in the medical profession. **C** Paul Campos, law professor and author of the 'Diet Myth', has even gone so far as to stick his neck out and question the link between obesity and mortality; a connection which has even been challenged by an article in the much-respected Journal of the American Medical Association (JAMA). **D** Author of the aforesaid article, Katherine Flegal of the 'Center for Disease Control and Prevention' (CDC), calls the severity of the dangers of excess body fat into question, indicating that the number of overweight and obesity-related deaths is actually about 26,000, about one fifteenth the earlier estimate of 400,000.

Reading Comprehension

1. The word **vociferous** in §3 is closest in meaning to
   a. noisy.
   b. objectionable.
   c. preposterous.
   d. consistent.

2. According to the passage, the link between obesity and disease is
   a. unequivocal.
   b. controversial.
   c. unpredictable.
   d. unlikely.

3. Why does the author refer to Paul Campos and the JAMA?
   a. as examples of well-known writers on the subject of obesity
   b. to point out shortcomings in the articles of both Campos and the JAMA
   c. to underline the current controversy over the link between obesity and illness
   d. as examples of controversial opinions that are now largely discredited

4. Which sentence below best expresses the essential information in the underlined sentence in §3?
   a. Intervention by authorities on the issue of obesity is underpinned by recent scientific research.
   b. Intervention by authorities on obesity is largely unwelcome because it is highly misguided.
   c. The long-awaited intervention of authorities on the issue of obesity has been catalysed by recent adverse publicity about obesity.
   d. The recent intervention of authorities on the issue of obesity was motivated by a public outcry.

5. All of the following are true about obesity **EXCEPT**
   a. it is an issue that is much debated.
   b. the issue of obesity is a strongly divisive one.
   c. it is an issue that has motivated authorities to act.
   d. people are less interested in the issue than previously.

6. Look at the four squares, **A**, **B**, **C** and **D**, which indicate where the following sentence could be added to the passage. Where would the sentence best fit?   Right Answer: A

   The latter is highly debatable, however.

7. An introductory sentence for a brief summary of the passage is provided below. Complete the summary by selecting the **THREE** answer choices that express the most important ideas in the passage. Some sentences do not belong in the summary because they express ideas that are not presented in the passage or are ideas of minor importance. **This question is worth 2 points.**

   There is no valid argument for recent intervention of authorities in the issue of obesity.

   a. The recent intervention of authorities has discredited the anti-obesity campaign.
   b. Government intervention has reignited the anti-obesity debate.
   c. Even long-held beliefs about obesity and illness are being called into question.
   d. Specifically, the link between fatalities and obesity is in doubt.
   e. Flegal, a respected authority on obesity, has challenged previously accepted figures on mortality and obesity.
   f. The incidences of obesity-related deaths look set to rise again.

Paragraph 4

Since it can be seen that obesity itself is hard to define and is erroneously linked to medical problems, it would seem that the intervention of authorities in the matter of obesity is not just intrusive but also **groundless**. Furthermore, even were there to be a proven link between illness and obesity and an ideal body shape to conform to, what right do authorities have to insist on taking control over an individual's life choices and lifestyle? <u>An individual is by definition, just that.</u> **A** A free person with the right to make their own life choices even if it is to the detriment of their bodily shape/health. **B** Infringement of such rights smacks of totalitarianism. Totalitarian regimes seek to control every aspect of an individual's life from religion to education. Controlling an individual's dietary regime surely is just one step removed from a Big Brother type scenario where the individual is but an automaton controlled by the state. **C** Interestingly, Paul Campo made the point, in his eponymous book, that the intervention of authorities in the obesity issue is not so much motivated by health concerns as by an underlying hatred of society for the obese. Now, that one might say is real food for thought. **D**

Reading Comprehension

1. The word **groundless** in §4 is closest in meaning to
   a. incompatible.
   b. undifferentiated.
   c. unsubstantiated.
   d. perplexing.

2. According to the passage, what has been the outcome of recent medical findings on obesity?
   a. It has incited fierce opposition amongst the medical profession.
   b. The link between obesity and illness is now untenable.
   c. It has promoted further research into the issue of obesity.
   d. There is now a strong mistrust of the medical profession.

3. According to the author, why is the intervention of authorities on the subject of obesity particularly distasteful?
   a. Such intervention opposes freedom of expression.
   b. Authorities have no clear strategy to combat obesity.
   c. Individuals become incapable of making informed decisions.
   d. The authorities themselves are not adequately informed on the subject of obesity.

4. Which sentence below best expresses the essential information in the underlined sentence in §4?
   a. It is hard to define the concept of 'individual'.
   b. An individual is simply not in control.
   c. An individual is someone who should act as described by the term 'individual'.
   d. The term 'individual' is easily defined.

5. All of the following are true of authoritarian regimes **EXCEPT**
   a. individualism is nurtured.
   b. freedom of expression is inhibited.
   c. they are all-pervasive.
   d. the individual is only a number.

6. Look at the four squares, **A**, **B**, **C** and **D**, which indicate where the following sentence could be added to the passage. Where would the sentence best fit? Right Answer: A

   No more, no less.

7. An introductory sentence for a brief summary of the passage is provided below. Complete the summary by selecting the **THREE** answer choices that express the most important ideas in the passage. Some sentences do not belong in the summary because they express ideas that are not presented in the passage or are ideas of minor importance. **This question is worth 2 points.**

   No identifiable link between obesity and illness renders medical intervention unnecessary.

   a. The intervention of authorities would be justified if a connection between illness and obesity existed.
   b. The intervention of authorities in individual matters is never justified.
   c. Since individuals are incapable of taking action themselves, the authorities have had to step in.
   d. Authoritarian governments exert stringent controls over the individual.
   e. Totalitarian regimes are not keen on gaining control.
   f. There is a hidden agenda in the anti-obesity campaign.

Paragraph 5

What really seems to be the issue therefore is that modern society finds obesity repulsive. This is the real reason behind anti-obesity campaigns. <u>Fat people just seem to be air-brushed out of society</u>. Any doubt that this should be the case is swiftly removed by a **cursory** glance at the glossy magazines on sale. **A** When was the last time you saw an oversize model, oversize meaning size 8 and above, staring out at you from the magazine racks? **B** Admittedly, Cosmopolitan made a brief incursion into the realm of the more 'generous sized' by displaying magazines with 'large' models and others with 'normal' models to see which magazine sold but this experiment was never repeated, presumably because 'large' doesn't sell. **C** So it is we as a society that is at fault. If we change our perceptions then maybe intervention on obesity will seem both irrelevant and unnecessary. **D**

Reading Comprehension

1. The word **cursory** in §5 is closest in meaning to
   a. critical.   c. brief.
   b. appraising.   d. unobtrusive.

2. According to the passage, what is true of oversize models?
   a. They are very much in demand.
   b. Such models rarely grace magazine covers.
   c. They are valued as they represent 'real' women.
   d. Many women see them as role models.

3. What does the author believe guides the selection of certain model sizes for magazine covers?
   a. model availability
   b. discrimination
   c. superfluous factors
   d. model fees

4. Which sentence below best expresses the essential information in the underlined sentence in §5?
   a. Obese models need more air-brushing when they are put on magazine covers.
   b. Fat people are invisible in contemporary society.
   c. Those who are obese are reviled by society.
   d. The obese have a fairly high-profile in today's society.

5. All of the following are true about Cosmopolitan's campaign to feature larger models **EXCEPT**
   a. the idea was motivated by financial gain.
   b. it proved a failure.
   c. it was an attempt to defy the norm.
   d. the outcome merely confirmed society's prejudice against the obese.

6. Look at the four squares, **A**, **B**, **C** and **D**, which indicate where the following sentence could be added to the passage. Where would the sentence best fit?   Right Answer: C

Sad, but true.

7. An introductory sentence for a brief summary of the passage is provided below. Complete the summary by selecting the **THREE** answer choices that express the most important ideas in the passage. Some sentences do not belong in the summary because they express ideas that are not presented in the passage or are ideas of minor importance. **This question is worth 2 points.**

Recent campaigns to tackle obesity are merely reflections of society's deep-seated hatred of the obese.

   a. People don't pay much attention to what obese people have to say.
   b. The obese have no visual presence in the media.
   c. Recently society has become less tolerant toward the obese.
   d. A well-known magazine tried in vain to defy societal prejudices.
   e. A sea-change in societal perceptions of obesity will lead to acceptance.
   f. Modern perceptions of obesity are likely to change leading to greater acceptance of the obese.

Debate 6

Debate 6

Paragraph 6

So it can be seen that government/school intervention cannot be justified at any level, from the purely aesthetic to the medical. **A** At best it can be seen as **meddling**, but at worst a more sinister attempt of the state to infiltrate the individual's life and very being to ensure absolute power and control over the individuals themselves. It would be laughable were it not for the message that such governmental intervention is sending out to us all: 'We own you intellectually but physically, too.' Political issues aside, such body fascism just makes for a society that is paranoid and miserable about its bodily image, with the knock-on effects of a lowering of self-esteem leading to a plethora of other problems both psychological and physical, anorexia being just one such example. **B** Isn't it time therefore that we made a stand against authoritarian meddling in our lives and became responsible for our own diet and daily exercise regimes? **C** So, pass me the cream cakes please. Oh and while you're at it tear up that government leaflet on 'Healthy Eating' that's just dropped on my doormat. **D**

Reading Comprehension

1. The word **meddling** in §6 is closest in meaning to
   - **a.** interfering.
   - **b.** assessing.
   - **c.** discriminatory.
   - **d.** futile.

2. According to the passage why is government intervention sinister?
   - **a.** It is unprecedented.
   - **b.** It seeks absolute control over the individual.
   - **c.** There are no stringent measures in place to control government intervention.
   - **d.** People are overestimating the extent of governmental intervention.

3. According to the author, ostracizing the obese results in
   - **a.** far-reaching mental and physical issues.
   - **b.** a more motivated society.
   - **c.** positive outcomes for society.
   - **d.** a decline in the numbers of obese people in society.

4. Which sentence below best expresses the essential information in the underlined sentence in §6?
   - **a.** It is high time we rebelled against government intervention and monitored our own diets.
   - **b.** Government intervention will encourage us to regulate our own diets.
   - **c.** We should welcome government intervention and take on board official advice on diet and exercise regimes.
   - **d.** Timely government intervention has made us all more diet-conscious.

5. All of the following are true about government intervention **EXCEPT**
   - **a.** it makes for a healthier, more diet-conscious society.
   - **b.** an attempt is made to assert control over the individual.
   - **c.** only negative outcomes result.
   - **d.** the effects on the individual are far-reaching.

6. Look at the four squares, **A**, **B**, **C** and **D**, which indicate where the following sentence could be added to the passage. Where would the sentence best fit?   Right Answer: C

   We have been walked over for long enough!

7. An introductory sentence for a brief summary of the passage is provided below. Complete the summary by selecting the **THREE** answer choices that express the most important ideas in the passage. Some sentences do not belong in the summary because they express ideas that are not presented in the passage or are ideas of minor importance. **This question is worth 2 points.**

   No justification exists for government intervention in the issue of obesity.

   - **a.** The insidious nature of government intervention means that it is to be mistrusted.
   - **b.** Dictating how an individual should look results in physical and psychological issues in the individual.
   - **c.** The government has a fundamental right to offer guidance to individuals in modern society.
   - **d.** It is quite comical, in a way, to see how the government has tried to inveigle its way into the lives of individuals.
   - **e.** We need to rebel against governmental control.
   - **f.** A few treats, like cream cakes, never did anyone any harm.

Obesity: Schools and/or Governments should Intervene

Obesity is an issue that pervades society. Rocketing levels of obesity, peaking in the US with 66.6% (about 200 million) of the population being categorized as being overweight or obese, mean this modern-day epidemic that is a scourge on our society has now taken hold in no uncertain terms. No longer can this issue be brushed under the carpet, since obesity and its concomitant problems affect us all, whether directly, if we ourselves or a family member is obese or indirectly in the increased taxes that we must pay to provide healthcare for the morbidly obese. Since obesity figures speak for themselves, affected individuals have been shown to be hopelessly inadequate when it comes to self-monitoring and implementing their own health and diet regimes. For this reason it has become mandatory for schools and governments to step in and take action and reduce the incidence of obesity in society.

Firstly, if one takes a look at the plethora of health issues arising from obesity, it becomes immediately apparent that sitting on the fence with regard to this medical problem, is no longer an option. Adverse effects arising from obesity range from diabetes to cardiovascular disease, infertility and cancer. Such a list is by no means exhaustive but is intended to convey the insidious and far-reaching effects that being obese has on the individual. In addition, an obese individual can expect to trim years off life expectancy, up to 6-7 years in more extreme cases. Adding to that grim statistic, it should be mentioned that obesity now causes 112,000 excess deaths in the US, according to a study published in August 2006 in the New England Journal of Medicine. Notwithstanding the physical problems that are a corollary of obesity, there are also knock-on psychological effects experienced too by an obese individual, ranging from loss of self-esteem to depression and eating disorders, such as bulimia.

Secondly, disregarding the effect of obesity on the individual and focusing on obesity and society, it is clear that there is a need for drastic action. The obese are a burden on the healthcare system which is already stretched to its limit both financially and from the aspect of healthcare, as limited resources are diverted to those who are ill largely through a lack of self-discipline with regard to diet and health regimes. As the comedian Ricky Gervais has so succinctly put it, whilst elaborating on the theme of obesity 'No, it's (obesity) not a disease, it's greed. You just love to eat.' Joking apart, such individual lack of dietary self-restraint has resulted in healthcare costs escalating and burdening the already financially-strained US healthcare system to the tune of $147 billion for the treatment of obese patients.

Given the fact that intervention is of paramount importance, the question is how best can intervention programs on obesity be implemented? Since research has shown that the tendency to be obese is laid down in childhood, through a combination of environmental factors, such as education, peer pressure and family background, it seems logical that the first step should be to tackle the problem at its root. Educational programs on healthy eating should be introduced from an early age to instill the importance of diet and healthy eating on impressionable young minds. Where such programs have been initiated, their success has been unequivocal: a school in Philadelphia, Pennsylvania, for example, reported a 50% reduction in the weight of obese students. At the end of the intervention program 7.5 % of students were overweight, compared with 14.9% in non-participating students.

Obviously, nipping the problem in the bud is better than addressing the problem of obesity in later adult life, when unhealthy eating habits have already become firmly entrenched. Nevertheless, adult intervention programs still yield encouraging results. Whilst some companies have taken it upon themselves to motivate employees to lose weight, through financial incentives, as is the case for example with some firms in Dubai and the US, in other countries, like Japan, the government has muscled in on the act and taken a hardline approach that has seen a reversal in the rising trend of obesity. Whilst some may blanche at their rather indiscreet approach (employees deemed overweight are subjected to annual waist-measuring by their companies) the program has seen obesity rates slashed to 3.5% as compared to 30% in the US. Japan is now the slimmest industrial nation, as good an argument as any for government intervention in the issue of obesity.

In conclusion, it can be seen that both school and government intervention programs have proved surprisingly effective. It flies in the face of logic to ignore the results and argue against such intervention. However, no one is advocating coercion in these methods of intervention. Obviously such intervention programs still require the co-operation of the individuals concerned, even the austere Japanese program punishes the company, rather than the individual, for non-co-operation, so ultimately participation is still the latter's choice. There is no excuse therefore not to allow the intervention of authorities in preventing obesity. We only stand to benefit from such intervention. To continue in the present fashion of indulging the overweight rather than exhorting them to lose weight will only result in increasing the incidence of obesity-related diseases in the population and burdening the health services and ultimately the tax-payer who funds such services even further.

Debate 6

Paragraph 1

Obesity is an issue that pervades society. Rocketing levels of obesity-peaking in the US, with 66.6% (about 200 million) of the population being categorized as being overweight or obese, mean this modern-day epidemic that is a **scourge** on our society has now taken hold in no uncertain terms. No longer can this issue be brushed under the carpet, since obesity and its concomitant problems affects us all, whether directly, if we ourselves or a family member is obese or indirectly in the increased taxes that we must pay to provide healthcare for the morbidly obese. Since obesity figures speak for themselves, affected individuals have been shown to be hopelessly inadequate when it comes to self-monitoring and implementing their own health and diet regimes. For this reason it has become mandatory for schools and governments to step in and take action and reduce the incidence of obesity in society.

1. The word **scourge** in §1 is closest in meaning to
   a. affliction.
   b. challenge.
   c. shame.
   d. problem.

2. Based on the passage, the author believes that the issue of obesity
   a. is an insurmountable problem.
   b. affects a minority.
   c. is an affliction of the working class.
   d. needs to be addressed.

3. The failure of individuals to control their weight has been revealed by
   a. an increased incidence of obesity in the population.
   b. the healthcare services.
   c. family and friends of affected individuals.
   d. school and government reports.

Paragraph 2

Firstly, if one takes a look at the plethora of health issues arising from obesity, it becomes immediately apparent that sitting on the fence with regard to this medical problem is no longer an option. Adverse effects arising from obesity range from diabetes to cardiovascular disease, infertility and cancer. Such a list is by no means **exhaustive** but is intended to convey the insidious and far-reaching effects that being obese has on the individual. In addition, an obese individual can expect to trim years off life expectancy-up to 6-7 years in more extreme cases. Adding to that grim statistic, it should be mentioned that obesity now causes 112,000 excess deaths in the US, according to a study published in August 2006 in the New England Journal of Medicine. Notwithstanding the physical problems that are a corollary of obesity, there are also knock-on psychological effects experienced too by an obese individual, ranging from loss of self-esteem to depression and eating disorders such as bulimia.

4. The word **exhaustive** in §2 is closest in meaning to
   a. irritating.
   b. tiring.
   c. complete.
   d. negative.

5. Why is there an urgent need to address the issue of obesity, according to the author?
   a. It has hitherto been considered of no importance.
   b. There is a general reluctance in society to act.
   c. It has far-reaching health complications.
   d. The effects of obesity on health have recently come to light.

Paragraph 3

Secondly, disregarding the effect of obesity on the individual and focusing on obesity and society, it is clear that there is a need for drastic action. The obese are a burden on the healthcare system which is already stretched to its limit both financially and from the aspect of healthcare, as limited resources are diverted to those who are ill largely through a lack of self-discipline with regard to diet and health regimes. As the comedian Ricky Gervais has so succinctly put it, whilst **elaborating** on the theme of obesity 'No, it's (obesity) not a disease, it's greed. You just love to eat.' **Joking apart**, such individual lack of dietary self-restraint has resulted in healthcare costs escalating and burdening the already financially-strained healthcare system to the tune of $147 billion for the treatment of obese patients.

6. The word **elaborating** in §3 is closest in meaning to
   a. expanding.
   b. commenting.
   c. ridiculing.
   d. referring.

7. Why does the author use the expression **joking apart** in §3?
   a. to indicate an amusing aside
   b. to focus the reader on a more serious issue
   c. in order to adopt a more light-hearted approach
   d. as an admonishment to those who see obesity as a laughing matter

Paragraph 4

Given the fact that intervention is of paramount importance, the question is how best can intervention programs on obesity be implemented? Since research has shown that the tendency to be obese is laid down in childhood, through a combination of environmental factors, such as education, peer pressure and family background, it seems logical that the first step should be to tackle the problem at its root. Educational programs on healthy eating should be introduced from an early age to instill the importance of diet and healthy eating on impressionable young minds. Where such programs have been initiated, their success has been **unequivocal**: a school in Philadelphia, Pennsylvania, for example, reported a 50% reduction in the weight of obese students. At the end of the intervention program, 7.5 % of students were overweight, compared with 14.9% in non-participating students.

8. The word **unequivocal** in §4 is closest in meaning to
  a. shocking.
  b. unambiguous.
  c. revelatory.
  d. worrying.

9. The author believes that intervention programs should focus on schoolchildren
  a. since patterns of eating are determined early on.
  b. because school food is rarely nutritious.
  c. as children are more interested in diet than adults.
  d. because adults have less time to devote to learning about diet.

Paragraph 5

Obviously, **nipping the problem in the bud** is better than addressing the problem of obesity in later adult life, when unhealthy eating habits have already become firmly **entrenched**. Nevertheless, adult intervention programs still yield encouraging results. Whilst some companies have taken it upon themselves to motivate employees to lose weight, through financial incentives, as is the case, for example, with some firms in Dubai and the US, in other countries, like Japan, the government has muscled in on the act and taken a hardline approach that has seen a reversal in the rising trend of obesity. Whilst some may blanche at their rather indiscreet approach, employees deemed overweight are subjected to annual waist-measuring by their companies, the program has seen obesity rates slashed to 3.5% as compared to 30% in the US. Japan is now the slimmest industrial nation, as good an argument as any for government intervention in the issue of obesity.

10. The phrase **nipping the problem in the bud** in §5 is closest in meaning to
  a. tackling a difficult problem.
  b. avoiding a complicated situation.
  c. stopping a problem from developing.
  d. identifying a problem.

11. The word **entrenched** in §5 is closest in meaning to
  a. resolved.   **c.** arranged.
  b. embedded.   **d.** implicated.

12. What does the author think of the Japanese program?
  a. It is unacceptably intrusive.
  b. The embarrassment involved justifies the results.
  c. Most people would be amenable to such a program.
  d. It fails to justify government intervention.

Paragraph 6

In conclusion, it can be seen that both school and government intervention programs have proved surprisingly effective. It flies in the face of logic to ignore the results and argue against such intervention. **A** However, no one is advocating coercion in these methods of intervention. **B** Obviously such intervention programs still require the co-operation of the individuals concerned, even the **austere** Japanese program punishes the company, rather than the individual for non-co-operation, so ultimately participation is still the latter's choice. **C** There is no excuse therefore not to allow the intervention of authorities in preventing obesity. We only stand to benefit from such intervention. To continue in the present fashion of indulging the overweight rather than exhorting them to lose weight will only result in increasing the incidence of obesity-related diseases in the population and burdening the health services and ultimately the tax-payer who funds such services, even further. **D**

13. The word **austere** in §6 is closest in meaning to
  a. severe.   **c.** lax.
  b. bizarre   **d.** unconventional.

14. Look at the four squares, **A**, **B**, **C** and **D**, which indicate where the following sentence could be added to the passage. Where would the sentence best fit?   Right Answer: B

That would be positively Draconian.

Paragraphs 1 to 6

15. An introductory sentence for a brief summary of the passage is provided below. Complete the summary by selecting the **THREE** answer choices that express the most important ideas in the passage. Some sentences do not belong in the summary because they express ideas that are not presented in the passage or are ideas of minor importance. **This question is worth 2 points.**

The shocking prevalence of obesity in modern society now necessitates school and government intervention.

  a. Obesity has many repercussions on mental and physical health.
  b. There is a universal reluctance to implement anti-obesity programs in schools.
  c. The most effective intervention programs are implemented in schools.
  d. Ultimately only the intervention of authorities will make a difference.
  e. A public outcry followed the implementation of certain government programs.
  f. Unfortunately, the intervention of authorities may achieve very little in the long run.

Taking the Exam

(1) The exam is administered worldwide on fixed dates in secure, Internet-based exam centers.

(2) In most centers, there are several opportunities each month to sit the exam.

University Entry Requirements

Universities typically require a score of between 53 and 80 for undergraduate entry. However, this varies from place to place. For example, Cambridge University, in the UK, and Yale University, in the US, both require a score of 100 (with Cambridge also stipulating a minimum score of 25 for each element). It is always best to consult the website of the particular institution to which you are applying to find out the entry requirements of that institution, or those of the particular course you wish to enrol in, as entry requirements are occasionally course-specific.

Validity

Your TOEFL iBT scores are valid for two years.

Scoring

(1) Each section (Reading, Listening, Speaking and Writing) of the exam is scored separately.

(2) The number of points received (for each section) is converted into a scaled score from 0 to 30.

(3) The combined total possible score is, therefore, 120.

Section	Score
Reading	0 - 30
Listening	0 - 30
Speaking	0 - 30
Writing	0 - 30
Total	**0 - 120**

Reading Section

The simplest way to think of marking these sections in a practice test is by allotting one point to every question, with the exception, that is, of summary and chart questions. Summary and chart questions should be marked as follows:

Scoring for tables

In order to earn points, you must not only select correct answer choices, but also organize them correctly in the table.

For tables with **5 correct answers**, you can earn up to a total of **3 points**, depending on how many correct answers you select and correctly place.
* For 0, 1, or 2 correct answers you will receive no credit.
* For 3 correct answers you will receive 1 point.
* For 4 correct answers you will receive 2 points.
* For all 5 correct answers you will receive the entire 3 points.

Summary Questions	
Number of Correct Matches	Number of Points
0/3	0/2
1/3	0/2
2/3	1/2
3/3	2/2